# The Magic of the Valley

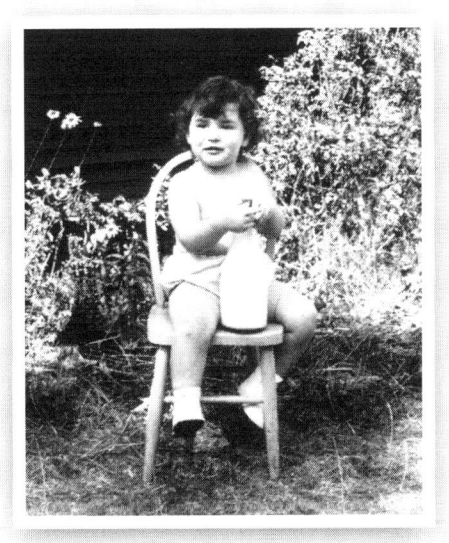

*The Life of* BILLIE HOWARD
*as told to* SUSAN PETTY

*The Magic of the Valley*
The Life of Billie Howard as told to Susan Petty
© 2014 by Susan Petty
First Printing November 2014

International Standard Book Number: 978-1-63452-313-4

Printed in the USA at Gorham Printing in Centralia, Washington

All rights reserved. No part of this publication may be reproduced, stored in a retrieval system or transmitted, in any form or by any means, electronic, mechanical, photocopying, recording, or otherwise, without the prior written permission of the author.

*In memory:*
*Dave James and George Hermes*

# Contents

Prologue ............................................................. vii

Chapter 1 ............................................................. 1

Chapter 2 ............................................................. 13

Chapter 3 ............................................................. 19

Chapter 4 ............................................................. 31

Chapter 5 ............................................................. 39

Chapter 6 ............................................................. 53

Chapter 7 ............................................................. 65

Chapter 8 ............................................................. 77

Chapter 9 ............................................................. 91

# Prologue

When Suzy Petty came to me to say she wanted to write my story, I thought she was nuts!

What have I done and where have I been? I could not think of anything worth writing about. I had read her book on Jim Carlton and loved it. I knew him, he was a good person, had a kooky sense of humor like mine, but he actually did stuff with his life.

Suzy brought it up again and again, so I gave in..thinking it would be about ten pages long.

Wrong! The sessions we had putting it together were something else. We laughed a lot and did some crying as well. I would have missed all that if I hadn't given in. Thank you, Suzy!

I dedicate this book to:

Dave James, past public relations person for Simpson Logging Company. I worked for him in 1957. He taught me the basics in writing articles and meeting and greeting people. I appreciated his sense of humor and ability to "schmooze" folks into telling their story. This trait served me well in my job as director of the museum.

And to George Hermes, the Principal at Irene S. Reed High School. When I was in high school, he scared me! He seemed gruff and stern.

*When I went to work for him in 1961 as a high school secretary, I learned to appreciate his ability to be tough when he needed to be and soft and easy going when it served the purpose.*

*I believe these two men helped me more in my career choice than anyone else. They both are gone now, but their memory lingers.*

*Billie Howard*

# WHITE GOLD IN COOKERY

BILLIE LEE LATZEL, GREETS YOU AT AGE 3

PRESENTED FOR YOUR CONVENIENCE BY

## LATZEL DAIRY

M. LATZEL, Proprietor

PHONE 215-J-2 — SHELTON, WASH.

NATURAL AND PASTEURIZED

MILK AND CREAM — BUTTER — BUTTERMILK

# 1

Many local folks just call it "The Skok." Officially it is known as the Skokomish River. This river, mentioned in the journals of Captain George Vancouver in 1792, originates in Washington State's Olympic Mountains. "Skokomish" means river people or "people of the river." The Skokomish were the largest of the Twana village community living along Hood Canal on the west side of the Kitsap Peninsula and the Puget Sound basin. The Skokomish Valley is approximately ten miles long, east to west, and nearly one mile wide, comprising the Upper, Middle and Lower communities of "the Valley." My family lived under the magic spell of this lush and productive valley.

My parents, Eva and Max Latzel, owned and operated a dairy farm in the Middle Valley less than a mile from the river. My dad delivered dairy products and fresh milk in clear glass bottles to the door steps of customers living on Hood Canal, just to the north of the valley. The farm had a herd of about fifty cows that included Jerseys, Guernseys, Holsteins, and a Black Angus bull named "Jimmy." All our bulls were named "Jimmy." My father loved that name. I am sure that would have been my name had I been a boy. Jimmy had a big ring in his nose. Daddy always told me that if that bull ever chased me, I should just grab and yank on that ring to make him stop short in his tracks. I never had the opportunity to experience just how that worked.

Two hundred apple and cherry trees kept Mother busy and my clothes stained with cherry juice. In addition to canning and baking the fruit, Mother would sell "U-Pick" apples and cherries for ten cents per pound. She would haul the old bathroom scale from the house to the porch for weighing the filled fruit boxes. She also sold cherries to a cannery in Tacoma. My parents were always working hard.

Our property had a barn, milk house, and a garage with a bunkhouse on top. Our farmhouse was larger than most in the valley. There were three bedrooms upstairs: one for my older sisters, Betty and Bernice; one for me; and the third for my parents. A huge walk-in storage closet at the top of the stairs held a large assortment of sheets, towels and anything else that could be shoved on to the shelves. The one and only bathroom, with a big claw-footed tub, was upstairs too. From my bedroom I could see our front yard and the adjacent road through the one big window flanked by a little

The Latzel Farmhouse still stands, just off West Skokomish Valley Road.

Dad, me, Mom, Betty and Bernice standing in our backyard.

one on each side. Almost every time I looked out my windows I would catch sight of Mother working on the flowers in the garden. I could see my swing hanging with two long ropes from a big old Douglas fir. There were blinds on my windows that Mother would pull down at night, and white gauzy curtains with ruffles on the top and bottom. A matching ruffled tie drew the curtains back to the sides of the windows. I preferred to have my windows open. My bed, a single metal one with springs on the bottom to hold the mattress, was up against the only solid wall in my room. On top of my bed was a white chenille bedspread with tassels around the edges. An enormous closet barely held all my stuff.

I particularly remember one morning on a Tuesday in November, 1940. I was five years old and had been asleep in my bed wearing my favorite nightgown. I did not like pajamas.

"Billie, time to get up," my mother commanded. I struggled to leave my comfy dream state. I'd been in bed for the past couple of days feeling sick. A high fever had me burning up and my body aching all over. Any food sounded awful. I really felt terrible. Mom figured it must be the flu. I did not like the fact that I wasn't feeling any better when I woke this morning.

"Let's get going, Billie," my mother said, standing at my bedroom door. I opened my eyes to see her wearing her best dress and goofy dark shoes with square two inch heels. She even had her favorite wide-brimmed felt hat positioned on her head. She always wore a hat when she went out. She was ready to go.

"Remember, it's Election Day today," she exclaimed, her voice revealing her excitement. "Finally we get to vote for F.D.R. Dad already milked the cows and is raring to go." She disappeared from my view to get her handbag.

Realizing this was a very important day for my folks, I grudgingly tried to stand by the side of my bed. Instantly I collapsed in a heap on the floor. "Mom, I can't move," I yelled in a panic.

"Oh, Billie, quit fooling around and just get up," Mother responded, convinced I was just joking with her.

"Mom, come quick. I really can't move," I cried. No matter how hard I tried, I could not make my legs move. They just stayed still, bent around me on the floor. I stared at them as if they were detached from my body. "Why can't I move you?" I tearfully whispered to them.

Mother walked in my room with that "Billie, you had better be up" look. That look immediately changed to an anguished "Uh oh. This isn't good."

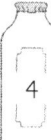

My big German father and little English mother carried me to the car post haste. They were exceptionally quiet in the car and drove rapidly to the nearest hospital, in Shelton. I guess we were all too afraid to talk. Our family physician, Dr. Collier, met us there and I was placed on a cold metal examining table. The doctor asked my parents lots of questions. He seemed puzzled about what could possibly be wrong with me.

He called in Dr. Kennedy to help him figure out what I had. The two of them talked to each other a lot. It was a long time for me to just lie there staring at the light over my head or glancing at everything in the spotless room. My parents looked more worried than I'd ever seen them be, even over a sick cow.

Finally the doctors decided to do something. A "spinal tap" they called it. As they started to play around with needles in my back, I was surprised I couldn't feel anything. I guess that is why it didn't hurt.

After the two doctors whispered to one another, they looked at my folks and said the word "polio." My mother gasped and my father took hold of her arm.

No one knew much about polio in 1940 and the doctors weren't exactly sure what to do or how to treat it. I was the first child in our neighborhood to get it. Lucky me. I am sure my doctors made the best decision they could at the time with the little information they had. They proceeded to construct a cast of white gauze and plaster from my little armpits to my ten toes as I watched in horror.

My father somberly carried me back to the car. My mother glumly followed with her head down looking at her shoes. I was now a little living mummy.

We weren't home for very long when I became very anxious. "Mom, I gotta go potty," I wailed.

They put me back in the car, and once again Father drove as fast as he could back to the hospital. We had discovered that Dr. Collier and Dr. Kennedy were not experts on body casting. They hurriedly cut a hole in my cast in the required place.

My parents did not get to vote for Franklin D. Roosevelt that year.

Father brought my bed from upstairs and placed it near the fireplace in the living room so I could be kept warm. I was now the household's main attraction. The wonderful smells from the adjacent kitchen filled my days. Mother always had a big pot of stew or something equally delicious cooking. And the scents of baking cherry and apple pies were heavenly. Every day smelled good. We were all thankful the polio had not struck my arms or my lungs, and that I could breathe.

I created clever ways to play and occupy myself. Gene Autry, the singing cowboy, was everyone's hero in 1940 and especially mine. For hours each day I would act out western fairy-tales with my prized plastic miniature cowboy and Indian figures. I made perfect mountains for them to climb, rivers to cross, and caves for them to hide in by cleverly folding and arranging my bed linens. Gene Autry always won.

Paper dolls were fun too. The perfectly shaped cardboard girls and boys had a large variety of paper clothes for every occasion. I would spread them out all over my bed. I had to be so careful not to lose the fragile costumes in the sheets or drop them on the floor.

I did not like sleeping in the living room at night. The house talked in creaks and snaps and moans that I had never heard before. Strange as it may seem, I do remember my dreams during this time in a cast. I flew like a bird in every one. I was always flying. Mostly I flew just like Superman, going from fencepost to fencepost across the neighborhood farms.

Using a bed pan was the worst part of my confined situation, especially since I was in the middle of the living room. My dear mother had to carry the used pan carefully up the stairs to empty it in the bathroom.

I really was never bored. I got lots of attention – and that part was fun.

My older sister, Betty, still lived at home but was absent most of the time with her busy high-school life. She did, however, sit and read to me often, which was cherished sister time. Her boyfriend, Bud Tozier, would stop over after work, put me in a wagon and pull me for long rides in the Valley.

Bernice, 19 and the oldest of us three girls, had been gone from our home for quite some time and was now attending beauty school in Bremerton. She generally considered me a miserable little pain and a dirty mess, running around everywhere as I did with skinned knees and food stains all down the front of me. Bernice was an accomplished piano player. Mother had all of us take piano lessons, but it was Bernice who proved to have the true talent. All through high school she frequently performed at concerts and plays. Now, when she did come home, I was delighted to be her audience as she beautifully played all the popular songs of the times.

Ella Mae Garrison, my playmate from up the road, came to see me sometimes. But her parents weren't very happy about it. People knew polio was highly contagious, and it didn't seem to matter that I had long passed the contagious stage: they still remained afraid their children would get it too. No one ever knew how I caught it, only that I had.

Dr. Kennedy and Dr. Collier came to our house to examine me and never spoke of me to others. We were very fearful that my father's customers would hear "polio" and be scared away even though it was tuberculosis, not polio, which could be transmitted between cattle and humans.

It seemed polio was in the news every day, or maybe that was just because I was living with it. Doctors knew very little about it, but were learning that

hot compresses and cold packs and some kinds of physical therapy might bring good results. After I had spent about one month in my cast, my doctors cut holes in it just below my knees so my lower legs could be massaged. I think that was very brave of them.

The doctors finally determined the cast could come off after a little more than three months, which seemed like three years. Oh so bravely, I lay completely still as they began the process. It was a time almost as frightening as having the cast put on! That funny round saw cutting through the cast all the way down my body: I just closed my eyes and hoped with all my might that I wouldn't get cut too.

Mother loved this hat! And I loved this dog!

I was shocked when my mother asked the doctor to give her that dirty, nasty cast to take home. Why in the world would she do that? I sure didn't want it.

It was quickly apparent that my right leg had not completely recovered from the polio. It was very weak and did not operate as it should. The doctors fitted a metal brace from my knee to my ankle. It was the latest in such a contraption and buckled right around my shoe. The doctors gave me crutches to help me balance and move the braced leg along. I adapted to the brace and crutches quite easily. Anything was better than being in a cast.

A few days later, Mother invited me out for an adventure. An adventure was never a part of mother's schedule. But on this day, Mother had something special she wanted just the two of us to do. She took me to our favorite spot on the river. We stood for some time just watching the water. Then, to my great surprise, my mother, with every bit of her might, threw that dirty, nasty body cast downstream! I must have been having too much fun to notice she had brought it with us. I watched that cast float away in shock and awe. I'll cherish that moment forever! The family never talked about my cast again.

Next the doctors told my parents that I needed physical therapy treatments and referred us to doctors in the downtown Seattle Medical/Dental Building. Mom had to drive me to Bremerton where we would catch the *Kalakala* ferry to Seattle and then a cab to my appointments. Riding the *Kalakala* was an experience by itself. It looked like something from outer space with all its silver metal and art deco style. And it would shudder and shake like crazy until it clicked into a smooth sailing gear. The inside was beautiful with a grand staircase leading up to the upper level. And there was a cafeteria, too. It was the coolest ferry I had ever seen.

Sometimes we would treat ourselves to a musical performance at the Moore Theatre. I can close my eyes and vividly remember the songs in *The Merry Widow* and the lively singing and dancing in *Carousel*. Or we would make a trip to the Pike Place Market before coming home. The fresh flowers there were always amazingly beautiful regardless of the season. Just people-watching was worth the visit. I remember these appointments as wonderful times together and the only times Mother was not working on the farm.

My mother did not have a driver's license. She had just never taken the time to get one, but she had been driving everywhere for years. While driving in the Valley one day, and directly in front of Patrolman Tom Kneeland, she unfortunately drove right through a stop sign. Patrolman Kneeland immediately pulled her over and asked to see her driver's license.

"I left it at home," mother quickly replied with her best smile.

"Mrs. Latzel, you don't have one, do you?" Patrolman Kneeland asked. I am not sure if it was her embarrassment or the price of the ticket that prompted Mother to become a licensed driver very soon after that encounter.

My mother, Eva Grace Ribbans Latzel, was an amazing woman. She was born in London, England, in 1900, the ninth child in a family of ten. At the age of twelve, she immigrated to Victoria, B.C. with her parents and siblings, except for two married sisters who remained in England. The family had a deep sense of faith and gritty determination. "Life is real, life is earnest," was a motto they embraced. Eva, my mother, went to work at thirteen years old darning socks and sewing on buttons in a laundry.

She met my father quite by accident when she was sixteen years old and visiting her sister, Rose Keir, and Rose's family in Washington State. Rose's husband, Harry, worked for the Seattle Coal and Fuel Company. As Eva was taking her baby nephew for a horse-drawn buggy ride, along came a young man with a team of horses on the same road. Wanting to get out of their way, she pulled to the side of the road, but her buggy toppled into a ditch. Max Latzel, the young man with the horses, came to Eva's rescue and pulled her team and buggy out of the ditch. Eva invited Max to dinner in Victoria, B.C. in gratitude for the rescue.

Max Latzel had sailed from Germany in 1906 aboard the *Carl*, a three-masted sailing ship, when he was fifteen years old. Deciding not to return to Germany, he left the ship when it was docked in Port Townsend. Max

worked in the farm fields prior to finding his way to Seattle and becoming a "wheeler," managing barrows pulled by a team of horses on new roads being constructed around downtown Seattle. He went to Ballard High School to learn English and lived in a boarding house for five dollars a week. Max managed to save fifty dollars with which he purchased his own team of horses and began his own business. He grew his business to six teams and hired out to the Seattle Coal and Fuel Company, delivering coal to apartments, hotels and private homes around the greater Seattle area. Rose's husband, Harry Keir, worked for Max at the Seattle Coal and Fuel Company.

Max became a U.S. citizen in 1916. A year later, America entered World War I and he was drafted in the first contingent. He trained at Camp Lewis for a short time. Max wrote to Eva often and visited whenever he could. Eva Ribbans married Max Latzel on April 26, 1919, in Victoria, B.C. They left immediately after the ceremony to make a home in Seattle.

Dad and Mom on the farmhouse porch during Latzel Dairy years

Demobilized, Max resumed his work for the Seattle Coal and Fuel Company with his team of horses and wagons. He and my mother lived in a small flat in the Rainier Valley. My father began to receive offers to work in Kitsap County, building roads and culverts with his horses and equipment. And soon he became involved in the logging business, which led him to Mason County. My father and mother then operated a hotel for a few years in Eldon on Hood Canal. Eventually they bought a home in the Middle Skokomish Valley and started Latzel Dairy.

Our dairy truck, sometimes used to deliver fruit to the cannery, driven by Bud Klink.

# 2

As far back as I can remember, I never hesitated to tell anyone my opinion – and I always had one. I must have been born with that trait, but my mother just called me "mouthy." I was curious about everything and loved

discovering. I can't remember ever getting upset about very much. And I never knew what a stranger was. I was on the small end of the scale for my age, and like most girls, had dark shoulder length hair that I wore in a variety of ways.

I tried to make polio a thing of the past, almost. I was mostly like other little five year olds, except for the brace and crutches. But I didn't let those things keep me down.

Everyone knew one another in the Valley. And they were happy. People worked hard

Ella Mae Garrison (left) and me

for their families and were always willing to give a hand to anyone who needed one. Several were dairy farmers also. The Garrison family of Ella Mae, two brothers, and an older sister, lived close. Ella Mae was my age, a skinny girl with long, curly brown hair. She had an older sister named Betty, just like I did. Ella Mae loved playing at my house. We would ride our big tricycles for hours all over the farm, romp in the barn hay, and go down to the river to play. We would dream up all kinds of amusing things to do together. We were adventuresome and clever, but never naughty or scared. Often Ella Mae's parents would resort to sending her older brothers to our house to bring her home. She loved to hide under my bed, somehow pulling her entire self up into the springs, so they couldn't find her. It was hard for me not to give her hiding place away.

Near the Garrisons lived the Bailey family: Zelda and Howard, Dale, Shirley, Marilyn, and Lorraine. The John Eager family lived across the road from the Baileys. My sisters, Betty and Bernice, were great friends of the Eager girls, Violet, Mary, and Sybil. They would trade clothing and jewelry from time to time. It was easy for my big sisters to bribe me into going over to the Eagers' house to try to retrieve their stuff. Most of the time I came home empty-handed. There were Eager sons too, Bob, John, and David. The Eager family was the only one I knew to have a root cellar. It was filled with potatoes, fruits and vegetables, and had stairs that went deep underground and a log cabin roof that sat on top.

The next farm down the road belonged to the Campbell family and their six children, Zanie, Cecil, Colleen, Rita, Jodie and Marilyn. The Campbell children loved to be barefoot and only wore shoes when absolutely necessary. The soles of their feet must have been like leather. The three boys wore bib overalls all the time. They were exceptional athletes in every sport. They played everything better than anyone else. The girls were exceptionally smart in every subject. They knew everything.

Adjacent to the Campbells lived Harold and Mabel Hunter, with Paul and Mary Hunter living across the creek. They were some of the first to settle in the Valley in the 1890s. They also had a large dairy farm and served areas of Mason County where our dairy did not. The Valley school teacher boarded with Harold and Mabel Monday through Friday in the early years.

And there was the Richert family. Mom always said that Dad was sweet on Ethel Richert. Dad always said Ted Richert had a big crush on Mother. Dad liked Ethel's potato soup. Mother never made any. One day, while I was still having to use crutches, my dad and I went to see Ted. Ted was in the barn milking his cows, so Dad told me to stay in the truck. Well, that wasn't any fun. So as I went to join them in the barn, I slipped on a pile of cow manure and fell right into the gutter. Dad was so mad at me that he refused to give me a hand and just watched me struggle to make my way out of that mess.

Every Sunday we had a lot of company. Mother usually cooked chicken in some form or another. Her favorite was chicken and dumplings and when she started throwing stuff in the pot, people just showed up. There were always a couple of delicious fruit pies too. My mother made the best pies! It was relatives who came the most. My mother's sister and brother-in-law, Rose and Harry, were always around. They had followed my parents to the Hood Canal area and lived in Shelton. And Harry's two sisters and their husbands came along too.

Of course, Mother always had to cook for the hired help as well. Her brother, Alf, and Rufus Wivell were the milkers. In the summertime we always had three or four high school boys from Shelton work in the hay, pick fruit, deliver milk and perform odd chores around the farm. They slept in a bunkhouse over the garage and ate at our table too.

As well as taking care of us, the hired help, the garden, the tree fruit and the cows, Mother knitted beautiful baby sweaters for every one of Dad's

expectant customers, and Dad always brought a bunch of fresh-picked flowers from our garden to anyone not feeling well. Mother somehow managed to teach me how to knit when I was quite young. I don't remember doing much knitting as a youngster, but certainly did as I got older, and still do today.

I am not sure exactly when Mother decided she loved birds. I do know that our house was filled with the sweet songs of 200 German roller canaries housed in a large walk-in aviary in the back yard that my father devised from a storage shed. Obviously, I would always wear a scarf on my head whenever I went in there. Mother loved her birds and cared for them tenderly. She would carefully place their tiny eggs in little boxes on the back of the stove to incubate. She knew just when to return the eggs to the nest to hatch. Mother belonged to a bird club and often participated in bird shows held in Seattle's Frye Hotel. Time and time again, her birds would win the coveted prize of "Best Singers." Mother named several of the birds. I especially remember Ozzie. He would sit on my finger and give me a kiss. People from all over the county would knock on our front door to buy one of mother's birds. Mrs. Callison, from Union, left with a bird one day but only after having tea with mother. Someone was always in our kitchen. I think the birds helped Mother keep her sanity. They certainly made her happy.

The pool at Sol Duc

The summer following my polio, and for many years thereafter, Mother rented a cabin at the Sol Duc Hot Springs on the Olympic Peninsula. My sisters and a few friends joined us. I would spend every day, from the time the pools opened until they closed, in that wonderful, warm, therapeutic water. Mom brought me sandwiches for lunch so I could stay in the water and not starve. That water was heavenly.

There is a memory prior to polio that speaks of my parents. I was about two years old when Mother's homesickness for her England got the absolute best of her. She had to return even if it meant leaving my father with very little me. Dear Mary Kneeland Shelton, daughter of Wallace Kneeland and sister to Patrolman Tom Kneeland, stepped in and took care of me sometimes so my father could continue his work. Mother stayed for about two months, getting a good dose of family, friends and England.

Since she was already abroad, Mother then decided to visit my father's family in Germany. It was 1937 and the Nazis had become active. Mother wrote about seeing the soldiers marching down the streets. Father was reading our news about possible war. He finally became so concerned that he sent a telegram to my mother demanding she come home immediately. Fortunately, she heeded his warnings and booked return passage. But Mother felt the necessity of buying a new pair of shoes for her trip home. When she told my grandmother and aunt in Germany that she planned to go to the shoe shop down the street, they immediately forbade her to do so. Inquiring why not, my mother was told it was because the owners of the shoe store were Jewish. World War II began immediately after her departure.

Middle Skokomish School photo in 1941. From left to right: Row 1 – Annette Bienek, Clara Markland, Billie Latzel, Delbert Moore, Patsy VanOverbeke, Bob Garrison, Janet Hunter, Roger Richert, Ella Mae Garrison, Delia Roberts. Row 2 – A Taylor boy, Zanie Campbell, Mitze VanOverbeke, Bill Stiner, Darlene Moore, Francis Johnson, Don Lyons, Ron Johnson, Jim Hunter. Row 3 – Mrs. Whitford, Gary Markland, Margie Dailey, Stan Johnson, Clark Butler, Bob Hunter, Jerry Richert, Leroy Moore, Clyde Simmons, Lavina Stiner, Patty Cox.

# 3

I was thrilled to begin school in the fall after the winter of polio. Our little local school, Middle Skokomish School, had only two rooms with three grades in each room: one for grades 1-3; another for 4-6. This building now serves as a community center and is owned by Skokomish Grange. In my days there, the building was really a busy place: school Monday through Friday; Grange meetings on Friday nights once a month; Grange dances on Saturday nights at least once a month with a midnight potluck followed by more dancing. The entire community was invited as well as members of other Granges in Mason County. This building was also used as a church and Sunday school until a church was built less than a mile from it sometime later. I attended Sunday school there off and on until 1948 when St. David's Episcopal Church was built in Shelton which then became – and still is – my church home.

I absolutely loved my time in grammar school. My first teacher, Mrs. Whitford, had grey hair, and was very sedate and nice. Mrs. Anna Berge, my second teacher, was a heavy woman who loved to play with us kids. She was excellent at organizing track meets and ball games. There were always school events supported by the entire community. The annual Christmas pageant was the most special. Every year each child received a beautiful cellophane bag filled with an orange, nuts, hard candy and candy canes. The magic of the Valley.

Early Sunday mornings, Bill Hunter would come to the school to pick up all the beer and liquor bottles left from the previous night's Grange party in preparation for Sunday's church services. Since liquor was not allowed in the building, folks did their drinking in cars and just threw out their bottles, knowing they would disappear by morning. Bill was a sixth grade "upper classmate." His mother, Mary, made sure he did the weekly bottle removal. On weekdays in cold weather, Doris Hunter, Bill's cousin, would come to school early to warm up the classrooms by building a wood fire in each one. She, too, was in the sixth grade. Her father, Harold, was on the school board. The value of community service was instilled in both Bill and Doris at a young age. (Bill went on to serve several terms as a county commissioner and Doris began her medical career as a missionary doctor in Africa. She returned to Shelton to work for many years as a trusted general practitioner.)

In the early days of the school, the bathroom was an outhouse that was customarily knocked over by the neighborhood boys every Halloween. That was not a community service!

The school was two miles up the road from our farm. There weren't any school buses and everyone just merrily walked together no matter what the weather. However, my teacher took pity on me with my crutches and leg brace and stopped in the mornings to give me a ride. Although I dearly appreciated the ride in the mornings, I didn't like waiting for her to grade papers and such after school, so I chose just to walk home with all my friends. We would stop and dilly-dally at each house. Grandma Hunter always had the best warm cookies waiting for us. And Mrs. Campbell always had lots of kids at her house, so play time there was great. Lorraine Bailey was my best friend, so playing at her house also was a must on my way home. I usually would arrive home just in time for dinner. But I guess I over-played once, as Mother came looking for me with a switch in her hand. I was shocked that she was mad enough to bring a switch – and she was still wearing her apron! How could she even think about switching me, her baby? She didn't – but she gave me a good scare!

I really did push my mother's buttons one day. World War II was still going on and Fort Lewis maintained an army camp in the nearby National Forest to patrol for Japanese aircraft. A huge army truck loaded with soldiers passed me on my way home from school one day. Taking pity on this poor little girl walking with crutches, they offered to drive me home. I was absolutely delighted and couldn't resist. But as my mother watched them hoist me off the truck in front of our house, she went ballistic. How could I, and why would I, put myself in such jeopardy, or something to that effect, is what she screamed at me. I didn't get why she was the most mad I'd ever seen her. I was definitely forbidden – in no uncertain terms – to accept a ride from anyone, and most especially young soldiers, ever again.

Annette Bienek was my first-grade friend. She was very smart and really good at baseball and running track. She lived in the Upper Valley so we were just friends at school. Delbert Moore was a good friend too. He had a hard time with learning but was the hardest working farm boy anyone ever knew. He could do anything.

When I was about seven years old, the polio doctor at Children's Orthopedic Hospital in Seattle, Dr. Wycoff, felt he should cut the tendon in my right foot. It had been "frozen," so I was unable to drop or raise my foot. Doctors had hoped the brace would have helped. The surgery, they said, might allow the foot to function more normally. There was quite a bit of confusion and uproar when we reported for our first appointment and were instructed to go to the boys' ward in Children's Orthopedic. No one thought a Billie could possibly be a girl! We spent uncountable hours getting to and from Children's Orthopedic Hospital, as well as just as many hours in the facility. Vivid memories remain of a playground on the roof where I watched children playing. Amazingly, I could walk better after the operation. I quit

A family portrait taken at the Latzel Home in Skokomish Valley about 1944 by George Andrews. Bernice is expecting her first child, Cathy, and is wearing a maternity dress.
Standing left to right: Arthur "Bud" Tozier, Betty Latzel Tozier, Bernice Latzel Moorhead, Trine Moorhead. Seated: Max Latzel, Billie Latzel and Eva Latzel.

wearing the leg brace and threw the crutches away. I learned how to throw my foot out and around, and was very much like all the other kids – finally.

At one point, my mother thought tap dancing would be good for me and signed me up. My right foot just flipped and flopped. I actually thought the whole ordeal was quite silly. I was not a tutu kind of girl and gave it up quite quickly.

I really preferred doing a lot of the things my dad did around the farm rather than what mom did around the house. I'd much rather clean the barn than the dishes! I liked the hay and the pitchforks. I was driving a tractor at ten years old and a milk truck at twelve. I loved to go on the milk route with my

Dad. We'd merrily sing songs along the way. I would get to meet his customers and talk up a storm. Those were my most favorite times with him.

I joined a 4-H club when I was about eleven years old. We would meet once a week at someone's home. The main focus of this club was, and is today, to teach and prepare young people to be able to explain themselves to an audience. My first project was learning how to sew both by hand and on a machine. My first assignment was to demonstrate the craft of darning at the county fair. I proudly held a holey sock over a light bulb in one hand and made perfect stitches with the other – perfect enough to win a blue ribbon. I was so impressed with Millie Dugger that year. She was a really cute girl from the Upper Valley who demonstrated how to wash a wool sweater. She did it using a couple of dishpans filled with water, and made a messy job look easy.

We were one of the first families in the Valley to have a telephone installed. Dad thought it was absolutely necessary for his business. Neighbors all

I am standing on the Fordson tractor that Dad, on the right, let me drive around the farm. That's the Latzel Dairy Farm bunkhouse in the background.

over the valley walked to our house to use this amazing instrument. One Thanksgiving, someone walked in anxiously asking my mother to call for help quick! A person at their dinner table had taken ill. In those times, there was no 911 service. The hearse and the ambulance were one and the same. The call was made, and my mother, being who she was, followed the woman back to her place hoping she could be of assistance until help arrived. Mother walked in to discover this poor woman's uncle had fallen over dead with his head in the mashed potatoes!

I graduated from sixth grade in 1946. To my dismay, my parents sold the Latzel Dairy and farmhouse. It had become too much for my 55-year-old father to maintain. I am sure that it was not an easy decision, but it was time. He sold most of our cows to Hunter Brothers Dairy and we moved to a smaller farm on Weaver Creek in the Valley. Dad took only about ten cows with us that he now milked himself, selling the milk to Kitsap Dairy in ten-gallon cans instead of glass milk bottles. Our move was only about three-quarters of a mile down the road, but it turned my life upside down.

Our square home. The faded extension on the left was added when my parents got older.

We now lived in a little two-bedroom, one-bath square house with a barn. And I started junior high school.

I'm not sure if it was the move or the new school that threw me. Probably both. Shelton Junior High School was awfully scary. Suddenly I went from the comfort of a two-room schoolhouse to a huge school where I had to change classes every hour. That was traumatic. And I had to be ready for the school bus each morning and board it promptly after my last class for the trip home. My life became very structured and scheduled for the first time. That part I didn't like at all. I was used to running around wherever I wanted and doing whatever pleased me at the moment just as long as I was home for dinner.

My neighborhood was different too. It wasn't as convenient for playing with my old friends. Although I still kept them as part of my life, I sought out new ones who lived nearby. Beverly Rosenberg, a year older than I, lived close on a berry farm. She and I would hire out to pick all kinds of berries. I never really got the hang of it so wasn't very good at it, but did manage to earn a few bucks. Beverly's grandmother, Hannah Peterson, adopted me as one of her own. She was the only "Grandmother" I ever knew and I loved her as I imagined a granddaughter would. That was a unique and cherished relationship for me.

Mr. Rosenberg took us kids Trick-or-Treating every Halloween, as long as we each had a flashlight. We would travel the same route every year visiting dozens of houses. Afterwards we all went to the Rosenbergs' house for a big party, where we dunked for apples, pulled taffy and traded candies.

And Clara Bourgault, my age, lived with her family across the river on a dairy farm. Her family was French Canadian and a bunch of fun-loving people who played a lot of barnyard baseball. You had to watch where you stepped. Most Friday evenings, Joe Bourgault would line the back of his truck with hay and fill it with kids. He would take us either to Twanoh State Park or Sandy Beach between Hoodsport and Potlach to swim and play for hours. What a wonderful way to end the day.

Forest Festival time brought in summer with a bang. The pageants were held on Loop Field during my junior high school days. Thousands of people would fill the football grandstand and bleachers to watch the school kids put on a play about Paul Bunyan. I danced in a square dance scene one year. School was put on hold for about three weeks in order for all the students to practice for and participate in the festival pageants. It was great fun.

There was always something to do. Baseball games were a highlight. Lucille Bourgault was old enough to drive. Neither one of us played baseball, so we would go to town and buy soda pop to resell to the players and fans. We always made enough to pay for the pop, but never any more.

My friends and I slept outside every night in the summer. We'd sleep in the woods, backyards, hay lofts, or wherever we got the notion to lay out our sleeping bags. We would sing songs, tell stories, count dozens of falling stars, and laugh.

When it was time to work the hay, everyone joined together. Men would help each other and share equipment; and the women served the workers huge meals. We kids pitched in and shared the load wherever we could. Folks borrowed anything and everything from one another. We were one big family traveling from one farm to the next getting all the work done. The magic of the Valley.

The Skokomish Indian Reservation had an excellent adult men's baseball team. The players even had their own uniforms. They traveled all over the Pacific Northwest playing and winning tournaments. Every Sunday, after Dad and I did our chores, we would go watch them play. We were two of their biggest fans. Dad was so impressed with them that he gave the team money to buy a wire backstop. The team thought he was a saint!

Emily Miller, a Skokomish Indian and neighbor, would walk from the Valley to Shelton to shop at Lumbermen's Mercantile for groceries. She would leave her groceries in the store and walk back, stopping at our house to visit and have tea with Mother. My father would then stop at Lumbermen's on

his way home to pick up Emily's bags of groceries, fetch Emily and drive her and her groceries home. This was their routine a couple of times a month. Emily was a fantastic basketmaker. I'm proud to have her baskets in my home today.

Emily had a son, Louie, who was known to steal now and again. One day Louie brought a big salmon to our house and offered to sell it to my father. Dad was impressed that Louie was trying to make a few bucks instead of stealing them, so he bought the salmon for five dollars. My mother took one look, and sniff, at that salmon and quickly buried it in the garden to fertilize her vegetables.

Photo courtesy Shelton–Mason County Journal archives

Emily Miller was one of the few Skokomish tribal members who practiced the art of basketmaking using traditional materials and methods. Materials used were cedar bark, sweetgrass, beargrass, cedar root, cattails and vine maple. Dyes were made from Oregon grape root which yields a bright yellow, alder bark for orange, cherry bark for red and special mud for black.

Another interesting basketmaker and Skokomish Indian woman, Louisa Pulsifer, had a grandson named Bill Smith, who had a friend named Gary Peterson. One day Louisa came to our door asking my mother if she could put these two boys to work. Mother did and discovered both Bill and Gary to be excellent farm laborers. I am friends with Bill and Gary to this day.

As I became a teenager, my world expanded. Every Friday night my parents went to Aunt Rose's house on Cota Street in Shelton for dinner and a game of pinochle. I would ride along with them only so I could join my friends to walk around downtown Shelton. It was the cool thing for us to do. I planned all week what I would wear to prance around downtown. You weren't cool if you weren't downtown on Friday night. We would meet other kids we knew and just loiter around and talk. I would end up back at Aunt Rose's house just in time to ride home with my folks.

Photo courtesy Mason County Historical Museum collection

Louisa Pulsifer taking a little break before she finishes weaving a basket during August of 1969.

I am guessing I am about ten years old here. I was so proud of my bike. I could ride and go anywhere I wanted. And did, for that matter.

# 4

I entered the tenth grade at Irene S. Reed High School. It was there that I discovered boys. I always had boy and girl friends and thought of the boys as just one of the gang. There were never any boyfriend-girlfriend relationships. We were just a bunch of buddies. But that was when I was younger! Now I looked at boys differently. They were so fascinating!

One particular Friday night while my girlfriend, Lucille, and I were gallivanting downtown, two guys in a very cool 1946 black Chevy convertible slowly drove by. Then they drove by again. Then they started to slowly

Irene S. Reed High School

Enjoying a lunch break sandwiched between two of my good friends, Arlene Berry, on the left, and Beverly Rosenberg, on the right.

follow us. Next, they were talking to us and inviting us to join them. Both had that electrifying "come hither" look on their faces. Lucille and I looked at each other with that "should we or shouldn't we" girlfriend query. The thought of riding around in that hip convertible was just too much of a temptation for two farm girls. I serendipitously jumped in next to the driver. Lucille liked the back seat. The driver introduced himself as "Frosty." The four of us had a blast driving around listening to "top ten" tunes, laughing and talking. Frosty made me feel special and I didn't want the ride to end.

Frosty was raised on a horse ranch in Colorado. He began riding horses before he could walk. Somehow a horse fell on him though, when he was nine years old. He suffered a broken back from the accident and spent a whole year in the hospital recovering. One arm was so badly damaged it never grew to the same length as the other. Several years later, Frosty was involved in a car accident and severely injured his leg. He wore a full brace on his damaged leg.

Maybe it was the brace that endeared him to me. Maybe it was his outgoing personality. Maybe it was his penetrating hazel eyes and infectious personality. Whatever it was, I was hooked.

Frosty, me, and the Chevy convertible.

Our dates almost always included dancing. Frosty was a fantastic dancer, with or without his brace, the kind of dancer that others stopped and watched, green with envy. I had enough rhythm in me – plus we were the same height – to make a great partner. We danced our way right into love. I was fifteen years old and Frosty was eleven years older.

Frosty had a large, loving family surrounding him. His sister, Bernice, and her husband, Roy Edwards, were the first to leave Colorado in search of work. When Roy found employment with Simpson Logging Company, Shelton became their new home. Another brother, Larry, followed in the same footsteps, leaving Colorado for Shelton and employment at Simpson. He married Betty Pierce. Much younger Frosty joined his siblings when both parents died in midlife. He also became successfully employed by Simpson, preparing samples of products for salesmen. Frosty enjoyed his job and was excellent at what he did.

I fell in love with his big family as much as they did with me. Because I was raised much like an "only child," my sisters being so much older and not an active part of my growing up years, I longed for the closeness of family. Frosty's family more than filled that need. And the family extended to include five nephews, a niece and many in-laws too. I embraced the family weekend potlucks. They were full of great merriment, dancing and singing. The adults of my new family often joined Frosty and me at Grange dances or parties. We were a couple strongly supported by friends and family. It seems quite astonishing that Frosty's sister and sister-in-law had the exact same names as my sisters, Bernice and Betty!

I was so connected with Frosty's family that they would call to make sure I was coming to the Saturday gathering, and tell me what to bring. I spoke with them more than I did with my own parents. Everything in my life went through them or came from them and definitely involved them. And, fortunately, my parents liked Frosty. He shared many good meals at our house.

Conversation around the table was easy with him, and Frosty was always happy around my parents.

On April 25, 1951, during a drive home from yet another one of his family's parties, Frosty said, "I have something for you," as he handed me a yellow gold diamond engagement ring. I was completely stunned. He and I had never talked about marriage. I had always lived just one day at a time without a thought of the future (and still do). I accepted the engagement ring simply as the next step toward being a part of this family that I loved. It was the spring of my high-school sophomore year.

I showed my engagement ring to my mother the next morning, which just happened to be her wedding anniversary. What an anniversary present I gave her! She wasn't totally surprised, but she wasn't exactly thrilled. In fact, she had a rather "drop dead" look on her face. I am sure she must have quickly reflected on being sixteen years old when she met my father; she had married him at nineteen. She probably would have married him earlier, but had to wait for him to come home from World War I. Truth is, she had been a much more mature teenager than I was, standing there with a silly grin on my face and an engagement ring on my finger. It took her about an hour to consult with my father and return with their response. They would give their consent to the marriage only if I agreed to register for continued education after high school graduation, and prior to the wedding. She was adamant that I should be self sufficient if I wanted or needed to be. Smart woman. Mother never mentioned Frosty in our conversation. And my father never spoke to me about my wedding. He and I didn't ever talk about personal stuff. We just had an unspoken understanding and quiet love for one another.

So at sixteen years old, I was in high school and engaged. Because of Frosty, most of my friends were adults. I acted as if I was one too. Somewhere I had left my childhood behind.

My life was changing fast. Frosty was too old to join me at school dances since people had to show their student ID card at the entrance. So I quit going to them. And Frosty was not physically able to climb the bleachers at the baseball games. So I quit going to them too. And besides he wasn't allowed to smoke at either one, and having a beer was definitely not allowed. That was that.

My father was still working for Kitsap Dairy. He never condemned me nor did he ever praise me. We were the closest when I rode in the truck with him to deliver to his customers. And Mom was still working as hard as ever around the Weaver Creek farm. I was in school, or with Frosty and his family, or working. And I was planning a wedding.

I worked at the Hoodsport Cafe as a waitress for Josie Lassoie on the weekends and whenever school was not in session. I loved this job and talking to the customers. They were mostly old folks who came in on a regular basis. Every Sunday at the exact same time, a huge Indian man and his wife arrived. He had incredible, massive hands that must have served him well as a horse logger. They were a sweet couple whom I always looked forward to serving. They never veered from ordering two fried-oyster dinners. The job at the cafe allowed me to develop skills in the art of conversation and dealing with the public. I was a responsible and respected employee.

I spent every penny I earned on filling the large cedar hope chest that Frosty had given me. Olson's Furniture, in downtown Shelton, gave an exact miniature of this chest to every senior girl for a high school graduation present. I had great fun shopping all the stores' sales and filling the chest with towels, sheets, two complete sets of dishes, silverware, and anything else that suited my fancy at the moment. But I never gave a thought to what marriage might be like.

In June of 1953, I graduated high school. I was ecstatic! No more P.E.! No more studying! No more tests! There was no celebration at home. It was done. It was over. And, giving me no options, my mother marched me into the registration office of the Dietz Business College in Olympia and signed me up for a secretarial/business course.

My senior photo

Irene S. Reed High School Class of 1953

# 5

Now, about the wedding.

I commissioned Mrs. Opal Clay to sew all the wedding ceremony dresses, all in exactly the same style and from the same cotton organza lace. I chose a classic floor length design with short sleeves and a scoop neckline. I was convinced that it was easier and cheaper if Mrs. Clay had to sew the same dress multiple times, just in different colors and sizes.

My oldest sister, Bernice Moorhead, gave me fits by not giving me a definite answer as to whether she was going to be able to make it to the wedding or not. She and her family lived on a navy base on the east coast, but it didn't seem to matter; she believed she should be the maid of honor. Finally I asked my sister, Betty, who lived just three miles down the road, to be my maid of honor, and she was thrilled. Betty would get to wear the yellow maid of honor dress. My bridesmaid, Betty Godwin (Frosty's sister-in-law), wore a pastel pink dress; Bernice was in pastel blue; Annette Bienek, my good friend, in pastel green; Arlene Berry, a close neighbor, in dark pink. Three little flower girls, nieces Maxine Tozier and Joyce and Cathy Moorhead, would wear white dresses that perfectly matched mine.

I never thought of the future beyond wearing that wedding dress.

Frosty had to go to Tacoma to find a custom tailor who could alter a suit to fit his numerous physical handicaps. He chose Ken Fredson, Bruce McLean, Larry Edwards, and Nat Stairs as his groomsmen, and Larry Godwin as best man.

My beloved soon-to-be family helped plan the formal wedding followed by a reception catered by Ken Frank in the Colonial House.

I insisted on being married in "my church," St. David's Episcopal Church, and we booked a date in July. Frosty and I were required to attend three pre-marital counseling sessions with Fr. Gardner, who met us at St. Andrew's House. We just took it all in stride. I was more worried that the priest would not like our eleven-year age difference more than anything else. But the priest just thought I was a rather mature "talker." I was more impressed

Standing left to right: Nat Stairs, Larry Edwards, Arlene (Berry) Smith, Bernice, Betty, Billie and Frosty, Larry Godwin, Bruce McLean, and Ken Fredson. In front left to right: Betty Godwin, Maxine Tozier, Joyce Moorhead, Art Tozier, Cathy Moorhead, and Annette Bienek (McGee).

by the incredible view of Hood Canal from St. Andrew's than I was with the counseling. Frosty was mostly frustrated that he was not allowed to smoke!

Looking back, it is all sort of a sweet blur of incredible nervousness. The church was full of family and friends. Ted and Ethel Richert were there, and the Hunters, Rosenbergs, and Bourgaults. It was a gathering of the Valley! My father stoically walked me down the aisle. The dresses fit perfectly and were beautiful. Everything went off without a hitch, except for a very young Art Tozier as the ring bearer. He fiddled with the rings until I thought he would drop them on the floor, never to be found. And just as Frosty and I were kneeling for the final blessing, a fretful Art cried loudly, "I need water. Water. Water. I want water now."

Me the bride in the middle surrounded by my sister Betty, on the left, and my sister Bernice, on the right.

Mr. and Mrs. Frosty Godwin

We were now Mr. and Mrs. Ralph Floyd Godwin. Hundreds of pictures were taken. Cake was cut and served. I changed my clothes and off we drove in that '46 Chevy convertible to La Junta, Colorado, to begin our honeymoon by visiting Frosty's grandma. We continued on to spend two weeks touring around Yellowstone and various tourist attractions. I took each day as an adventure.

We returned to a small square box of a house – or rather bungalow – in Shelton that Frosty had rented in preparation for our married life. He had taken the initiative to furnish it, albeit without consulting me. There wasn't a TV, only a radio. My filled hope chest was all I got to contribute.

That was it. I was a wife waiting for my husband to come home from work. And I was absolutely and completely and totally bored. The hours of each day seemed to last forever.

Fortunately for me, our home was situated directly behind Dr. Linkletter's clinic. So when Frosty went off to work, I could fill my days with watching the activities of the comings and goings of the clinic's patients and doctors after my chores were done. Or I would walk to town. Sometimes I'd just sit and read magazines all day. I always had dinner ready, and thankfully, Frosty ate everything I prepared. Weekends were wonderful as we joined family for fun, food and games.

I could hardly wait for secretarial/business school to start in September.

Finally, after dropping Frosty off at work, I happily drove to Dietz Business School, with Paralee Pace and Pat Hunter joining me. The three of us carried on and laughed all the way. Pat had the most infectious laugh of anyone I knew. I loved my classes and took to Gregg Shorthand like a duck takes to water. I had two years of typing in high school so had mastered agility with my fingers. My teacher, Everett Bell, was impressed by how quickly and painlessly I learned the squiggly abbreviated characters of shorthand. It wasn't long before I could take dictation at 120 words per minute. I translated my shorthand to business letters on a Royal manual typewriter with the letters blacked out on the keys so I couldn't look to find the alphabet.

The school received an application from a woman who was confined to a wheelchair. Classes were held upstairs and the building did not have an elevator, yet the school wanted to accommodate this applicant. She was my age and paralyzed from the waist down as a result of polio. Mr. Bell asked if I would be willing to drive to her house and teach her shorthand. I was delighted and went there every day for an hour and a half. This experience definitely deepened my gratitude for my polio recovery.

My evenings were now filled with practicing shorthand and studying. I constantly made shorthand symbols in the air with my fingers while listening to the news. That drove Frosty nuts! The Department of Vocational Rehabilitation completely paid my entire tuition because of my work limitations due to polio. Going to school was not a financial hardship nor did it require Frosty's money. Married life settled into a rhythm: Frosty went to work and I went to school.

But then Simpson decided to go on strike. Frosty had no job to go to and we had no money coming in. I was thrown completely off balance as to what to do. I wasn't ready for much of anything that was happening in my marriage. With no other options before us, we packed up the contents of the little house and moved in with my aging parents on the farm. Good grief!

I kept driving our only car to school as I wasn't about to miss any classes. My parents just kept doing what they always did. Frosty, with his friend and co-worker, Nat Stairs, went door to door trying to sell light bulbs. At least Frosty was busy doing something. I'll give him credit for that. I think he made about enough money to buy the gas for me to get to school. The strike lasted a very long, long three months.

Finally when the strike was over and Frosty was able to go back to Simpson, we moved in to a little one-bedroom house on Arcadia Street in Shelton. It was a cute house with a big backyard.

After eleven months, the school surprisingly committed me to a job. I hadn't even graduated yet, but I was deemed capable and qualified. I was extremely honored. So in 1954, I went to work as a secretary for the State of Washington Institutional Farm and Food Department. I was overjoyed! I worked for Carl Gilmore, head of the Farm Department, who was such a nice man; and Goldie Manning, head of the Food Department, who was as flamboyant as they come. I accompanied both managers to meetings in mental hospitals and correctional facilities. What an incredible experience that was. I particularly remember the huge Holstein cow herds one institution kept. I was fascinated by every facet of this job, especially the opportunity to communicate with people in all aspects of business. I was surrounded by men and women dressed in professional suits. I found learning about the operations of facilities captivating. I also embraced the tremendous organizational skills required of my job. It was gratifying to perform at such a high skill level. I quickly earned the respect of my coworkers and superiors. I was learning about me and I liked what I was becoming.

And I absolutely loved shopping on my lunch hour at M M Morris Dress Shop in Olympia. Or I would shop in Shelton at "LM," Lumbermen's Mercantile, that advertised "everything from a needle to a locomotive." This amazing store took up almost an entire block downtown. Looking professionally sharp was a definite requirement of my job. I wore the latest suits, dresses, skirts and jackets… and two inch heels. Polio was way in the past with no visible signs showing anywhere.

I made many new friends at work. We had a lot in common. We enjoyed each other and would spend time together away from work. There went my world, changing again. Frosty was not interested in my work friends, and did not like the time I spent with them.

One day I discovered I was pregnant. I did not plan it, but I didn't not plan it either. Both Frosty and I were perfectly fine with it. I wasn't sick one single morning and enjoyed an easy pregnancy. Wearing stylish maternity clothes, I continued working until the legal limit of six weeks prior to my due date.

Frosty decided we now needed a dog. One day he came home with a Boston Bull puppy named Susie that he bought from Mud Clay (whose wife had sewn the dresses for my wedding). Frosty thought I needed the company! Susie would not stay home and wandered the neighborhood. So, very pregnant, I had to walk all over and yell for Susie. What I should have realized was that if I just walked home, she would simply follow me.

Our son, Robert, was born in July of 1955 at Shelton General Hospital. He was the cutest baby I'd ever seen. I instantly fell head over heels in love with him.

My sister Betty gave us the baby bassinet she had used for her children. It was all fancied up with a new skirt and trim. I loved the fact that it had rollers on it. Mother knitted dozens of baby "soakers" from heavy white wool to put over the white flannel diapers she had sewn. And she supplied me with plenty of knitted blankets, baby hats, booties and sweaters. Planning for the future, she knitted

Mother's knitting pattern for baby clothes taken from Nursery Styles for 3–12 months by Beehive.

Evan Tozier on the left and Bob wearing their Mary Maxim sweaters.

Mary Maxim sweaters with colorful characters such as an English Beefeater, a brown fawn, and a yellow duck.

I was a wee bit nervous as a new mom, but my mother was only ten minutes away and eager to give a hand. And she overwhelmed me with dozens of "old wives' tales" on how to handle a baby.

Little Bob fussed every night at dinner without fail. I would put him in the baby basket and position it on the floor near the dinner table. I would eat and rock the basket with my foot, soothing Bob for at least a few minutes of peace and quiet.

Around the time of Bob's birth, Frosty and I bought our first home at 2036 Laurel Street in the Nash Addition to the Mountain View neighborhood in Shelton. I think we paid the huge price of about $10,000 for it. It was what young families were supposed to do.

I loved being a mother, but both financially and emotionally, I needed to go back to work. And, admittedly, I had a deep longing to return to the stimulation of the business world. At first, Joyce Jackstadt came to our house on a temporary basis to take care of Bob. Then, thankfully, I found Theda Jackson down the street. She was a sweet, motherly lady who was delighted to babysit Bob in her home. I felt confident Bob would be well taken care of by Theda and that gave me peace of mind.

So after six weeks of motherhood I returned to work. My prior job had been eliminated due to restructuring of the department, so I was asked to take a secretarial position with the Department of Youth Services, Juvenile Corrections Division. Ove Kilgren was a nice boss, albeit a little stuffy. I worked in a room with two other secretaries. My job mainly consisted of writing reports for the counselors working in the field. They were a bunch of great folks with wonderful attitudes. Even though this job wasn't quite as exhilarating as my previous one, it was a good one and fulfilling to me personally.

My father finally retired. He and Mom became devoted grandparents to Bob, and I enjoyed having them close by.

Bob was baptized at about three months of age, as was the custom of the time. It was a small ceremony at St. David's. He wore a long lace gown that my Mother had brought from England. My sisters' children had worn it also. It was absolutely gorgeous, although not too conducive to holding a squirmy baby in my arms.

One day Frosty decided our young son needed a horse. So he came home with Star—named because of an irregular star on his forehead. He was a sweet but feisty black-and-white Welsh pony. We really didn't have room for him so kept him at my folks' place when he wasn't visiting us. He would nip and kick a little if he didn't like something, but was so loveable. He had a liking for ladies, but not so much for gents. When Frosty got on his back, he would crow-hop around for a few minutes before settling down. One day when Star was visiting us, someone left the back door open. Star walked himself up the back steps into the laundry room and through to the small kitchen. There he just stood, watching me wash dishes with his big brown eyes. What an experience to turn around from the sink to face a horse! There wasn't room enough in the house for me to turn Star around, so I just led him through the living room, out the front door, and down the front steps to the yard.

Well, now my life was really changing. I didn't have much time even to think with the routine of work and being a parent. We still saw the usual "family gang," but not near as much as in the past.

Maybe it was because of having a son, maybe not. But deep inside I was feeling the pangs of missing my own short-lived childhood. Seems I had gone from being a carefree, independent, fun-loving child to a responsible adult and parent in a flash.

Every Sunday I took Bob with me to church at St. David's. Church was, and still is, a vital part of my life. Frosty wasn't interested. I envisioned Bob in a 4-H club and wanted him to have that experience. There wasn't one available, so I formed one with my sister Betty. I loved being a part of planning this, organizing, gathering people and accomplishing our goals. Frosty did not want any part of it and resented the attention I devoted to 4-H.

Just when six-year-old Bob started school in 1960, I gave birth to his sister, Eva. I was delighted when I heard the words "it's a girl." Named after my mother, she was a beautiful bundle of joy. And once again Mother supplied me with diapers and soakers. There were plenty of pink booties and sweaters too. I had time alone to bond with Eva while Bob was in school. And when Eva was six weeks old, I wanted to return to work for the same reasons as after Bob was born. I was grateful that wonderful Theda Jackson also welcomed Eva into her home. She loved my children nearly as much as I did.

When Eva was about three months old, we had her christened at St. David's wearing the same dress that Bob had worn. She was just as fussy as her brother was, so I also had to rock her during dinner.

Once again, just as I was ready to go back to work, I found my job eliminated by the state. Lucky for me, David James, public relations administrator for Simpson Timber Company, needed a secretary and I was hired. He was a great guy and a wonderful boss. My passion for writing was born with this job. I welcomed the challenge of writing articles for publication. Dave encouraged and tutored me well. I was very sorry when this job was eliminated, again due to re-organization, and I was re-assigned to the sales department. Eventually this position was also eliminated. Business was changing everywhere.

But I took the loss of my job as an opportunity to draw unemployment and stay home with my two children. It was actually a good time. I was as happy as I could be playing with Bob and Eva, and doing all the things I wanted to do.

The Unemployment Department required me to seek employment actively, which I did half-heartedly. Then one day I received a phone call from George Hermes, principal at Irene S. Reed High School. He had heard that I was unemployed and asked if I would be interested in a part-time job in his office. I'd had the opportunity to work for him during my high school years and jumped at the chance to do so again. Only this time I would actually earn a salary.

Bob holds Eva, dressed in her christening gown, with faithful Susie at his feet.

I happily went to work assisting George's full-time secretary. It wasn't long after I was employed when the secretary was forced to leave her job due to a serious illness. I then joyfully slipped in to her position.

Bob leading Star and Eva

Bob was doing well in school. He was also learning how to play the trumpet. He was old enough to stop at home to fix a peanut butter and jelly sandwich, or some such snack, after school before going to Theda's for the rest of the afternoon. One day Bob found our house full of steam and, in a panic, quickly ran next door to Mary Helser's house. Mary came over and immediately called the fire department first, and me second. Our water heater was about to blow up and the problem was easily addressed. But after rushing home from work and not finding Bob, I anxiously asked Jim Cross, the volunteer fireman, where my son was. Jim informed me that Bob had bravely saved his dog by running to a ditch across the road where he was sitting with one arm tightly around Susie, and the other arm clutching his cherished trumpet.

The seams of our house were splitting with two children, so Frosty and I sold the house on Mountain View and bought a larger, three-bedroom farm house on Arcadia Road on 4.5 acres for about $13,000. We were able to bring Star home from my parents' place to our own yard and his own barn. That stinker would escape every night, and every morning I would get a call from our neighbor asking if I could please come get the horse. I would drive the car for about a quarter of a mile, then lead Star home holding the rope out the car window. It was almost a daily routine.

The kids attended Southside School and our life became full of good neighbors. Ann and Ray Wheeler lived behind Bob and Anita Nault who lived beside us. And the Emsleys, an older couple, became grandparents to us all. And there were Lynn and Don Wilson across the road, too. I had graduated with Lynn from high school in 1953.

When Eva was about five years old she decided she just had to have a pet hamster. Frosty gave in to her demands and brought a small one home, complete with cage. Eva was good at keeping the hamster in the cage when she wasn't playing with it. But one day while Eva was playing with the little hamster upstairs in her room, it managed to slip into a very narrow space where the floor met the wall in her closet, and fell between the 2x4s to the floor below. That hamster scratched all night long trying to get out of his predicament, driving us all crazy. Frosty had no choice but to rescue the hamster by cutting a small hole in the wall and reaching in to grab it. A night not to be forgotten.

I loved my job at the high school. I knew just about everyone by their first names. I was thrilled when the Irene S. Reed High School Class of 1966 dedicated its yearbook, *Saghalie*, to me. How great was that!

My yearbook–dedication photo

However, by now my marriage had become one in name only. At least for me. Frosty seemed quite content with his daily routine. I had filled my life with my children, a job I loved, church, lots of new and old friends, plus activities that stimulated and fulfilled me. Frosty and I had grown far apart with nothing in common except the children. There wasn't any anger… there just wasn't any anything anymore.

So, one day I finally got up the nerve to tell Frosty that I was filing for divorce. I wasn't afraid. I really wasn't all that sad. It was what it was, and it was going nowhere. Eva was six years old and starting school. Bob was twelve and active in both school and 4-H. And they supported my decision. Realizing there was no turning back and accepting my resolve, Frosty reluctantly moved out of the house.

# 6

I felt an enormous sense of freedom – and great fear financially. My take-home pay was $350 a month that I could barely stretch to cover expenses. My parents were wonderful in helping me and feeding us. Bob took on the chore of chopping wood and bringing it in the house. He earned money mowing lawns. He quickly became a very responsible boy.

Bob and Eva alternated spending weekends with their father. Frosty took Bob hunting and fishing, instilling a great love of the outdoors. Eva learned how to act in a restaurant and order food, giving her a knowledge and appreciation of good cuisine.

My dear mother cleaned Frosty's house every week in her attempt to help him adjust!

The children and I were very active in the 4-H program, which continued to be a large part of our lives. Bob loved entomology and anything that had to do with bugs. I was always finding worms and other creepy things in his pants pockets. Eva's interests were in sewing and cooking. Demonstrating how to make Indian frybread, she won a "Best in Show" ribbon at the Puyallup Fair.

I went to the Panhandle Lake 4-H Camp every summer with my kids. That will always be one of my favorite-memory places. One year, when I was

Campers proudly raising the flag at Panhandle Lake 4–H camp.

the only adult counselor with fourteen kids, there was a wildfire not too far away. Fire department personnel told us we could be in danger if the fire spread and ordered us to evacuate. I had one car and fourteen lives to save. So I shuttled as many young campers and gear as my Chevy station wagon would hold at one time to the courthouse in Shelton, where parents could retrieve their youngsters. I am not sure how many trips I made back and forth, but we all survived. That was the end of that camping session.

And I went dancing! Every Saturday night Ann and Ray Wheeler, Bob and Donna Nutt, Lynn and Don Wilson, and I would find a country western band and kick up our heels. The Buzz Tavern was one of our favorite spots, but we liked Characters' Corner too. I dressed in a skirt of some sort and always wore high heels. I danced my best in heels! We would stop on our way home at Mac's Corner for the greatest hamburgers in town. But no matter what time I got home, the kids and I went to church the next morning.

Marilyn Lear came into my life about this time. She was a friend of a friend and we hit it off immediately. She was staying with her parents in Shelton while her husband, Charlie, was stationed in Vietnam with the Marines. Her two children, Etienne and Charlie, became friends with my children. We spent a lot of time together and it was quite comforting to have a friend I could relate to easily. She and her kids had just driven from North Carolina in a station wagon that could go farther on an empty tank of gas than anything I have ever seen. We hit some of the high spots as well as low ones, and laughed through them both. Marilyn fit so well into my Arcadia neighborhood that she became part of "the gang." She became a member of Saint David's church, and we went regularly – athough our halos could have been a little tarnished. When her husband returned from Vietnam, they returned to the base where he was stationed.

One summer my two nieces came to stay with me. Both had graduated from high school and were working in Olympia. Joyce was my sister Bernice's daughter, and Maxine was Betty's. I had more fun with my nieces than I ever had with my sisters. We all went to movies and shopped everywhere. One of our best times was going to the Seattle SeaFair Aqua Follies at Lake Union. We laughed at everything all the time.

So the kids and I were doing great and could hardly be any busier with all the activities we loved.

A couple of years as a single mom had passed when a co-worker, Carole Howard, asked me to join her to meet her brother-in-law at the Pine Tree Cafe. I thought it sounded like fun, so I accepted her invitation. Carol introduced me to Don Howard, and proceeded to do all the talking for the rest of the evening. Don left a so-so impression on me and I figured him to be a "pickup truck" kind of guy. A few weeks later, Don called and asked me to accompany him to Carol's daughter's wedding. "Why not?" was my reply. I would describe that date as "square." It was pleasant, but not terribly exciting. I ascertained that Don was a solid person with no quirks. But I also knew I wouldn't mind seeing him again.

I admit I had been looking for love, or something like it, in all the wrong places. Don was quite different from the few men I dated. He made me laugh. He was comfortable and honest. He was the "real meal deal." I knew in my heart that he was special and right for me. In fact, he was more than I could ever have imagined.

Well, Don and I starting dating and fit together like two peas in a pod. My family and neighbors quickly came to love him. He would visit his Aunt Lena and Aunt Neva in Montesano every Sunday. These wonderful elderly ladies lived in separate homes near each other. He took me with him one Sunday, and as we walked into Aunt Lena's house, she sweetly asked Don, "So is this your grass widow?" And Don proudly replied "Yes!" That name (an old slang word for a divorced woman) stuck and his family endearingly called me that while welcoming me with open arms.

Don was a forty-two-year-old who had never walked down the aisle. Coming from a hard-working family, he had learned how to be a timber faller at a young age. After graduating from college with a degree in psychology, he spent two years in the Army, after which he couldn't wait to return to the forest. He started Howard Cutting in Mason County. The company successfully grew to a crew of six men. Don knew his forest.

Don was a soft-spoken man with a quick and sharp wit and a passion for puns. People loved just being around him, sometimes only to hear what would come out of his mouth next.

Bob and Eva became comfortable around Don. Soon we were a foursome at dinner. Don would come to our house every evening after working all day in the woods. He'd drop his large metal lunch box on the kitchen counter and, wearing a silly grin, wait for me to open it. I always found a surprise or something for dinner. I might find three or four grouse, clean as a whistle and ready to cook. Sometimes it would be full of delicate chanterelle mushrooms. I loved when it was packed with juicy wild blackberries. Don was the best berry picker I had ever known. Whether it was grouse, mushrooms or berries, Don never told anyone where he found them. Those were his best-kept secrets.

Don and Bob went hunting, fishing and hiking as often as they could. And Don was attentive to Eva's involvement in 4-H and school activities. When Eva marched as a majorette in the Lake Fair Parade one year, and was completely exhausted from marching about four miles from Capitol Way to the Olympia waterfront, Don carried her on his back to the end of the parade gathering spot.

Bob and Eva also continued their relationship with their father. Their lives were full of love and balance.

Every evening after dinner Don would kiss me goodnight and then go home to his place in Hoodsport. He and I would have great dates on the weekends, mostly attending neighbors' potlucks or going dancing. No matter what the occasion, Don and I were together. My daughter, Eva, announced to me one day that she and "Grandma" (my mother) thought that Don and I should be married. They were that confident in our love and I was too.

So I started thinking that I wanted more than this steady-date relationship with Don. I began to rehearse a script in my head and even practiced it out loud a few times to test how it sounded. When I was good and ready one night after dinner, I told Don that I was sick and tired of this going steady business and he had better pee or get off the pot. He quickly and calmly replied that he didn't want to live without me and since he couldn't live with me, then we had better get married so he could. Then he kissed me goodnight and went home!

In the midst of planning our wedding, Don broke a few ribs and a cheekbone in a logging accident that landed him in the Shelton Hospital for a

few days. I went to see him, and surprisingly found him in the maternity ward – much to his chagrin. The hospital was so crowded that was the only place they had an empty bed. That was worth quite a few laughs.

On December 26, 1970, Don and I were married by Father Don Maddux in St. David of Wales Church in Shelton, in front of a large gathering of family and friends. Both my children were part of the wedding. I beamed with delight, as did my father, as he walked me down the aisle. And all my Valley friends were in the church pews.

But two days before the wedding, Don and I suddenly realized we had completely forgotten about buying rings. He did not want to wear one for fear of it catching on logging equipment, but we needed to buy one for me. So off we rushed to J. C. Penney's in the Tacoma Mall on Christmas Eve. We could only find a wide band that was my size and acceptable to us. We bought that ring and Don vowed to someday replace it with a fancier

Left: A beaming Eva standing between my father and mother. One could have thought it was her wedding! Right: Bob proudly served as an acolyte for our wedding ceremony.

one. I wore that plain band for nearly 40 years.

We cooked all Christmas day, preparing the food to serve at our wedding reception in Memorial Hall. Don and I never even got a taste as every bite was eaten by our guests. Everyone had a great time. People were so happy for us. And we were too. Afterwards we traveled down the Oregon Coast for our honeymoon, stopping to visit Don's aunt and uncle in Salem. It rained the entire time. We didn't care.

Don moved into my house on Arcadia and finally didn't have to leave after dinner!

Mr. and Mrs. Don Howard

The four of us settled into a sweet life of family, neighbors and friends. Life was the best I had ever known it to be. Everything seemed to make sense now.

It didn't take money for us to have fun. Our wonderful neighbors – the Wheelers, the Naults, the Emsleys, and the Wilsons, always had something going on. There was a potluck every weekend at someone's house. What one wouldn't think of, someone else would. We ate, we played, and we laughed a lot.

Don did all the things I hadn't done and couldn't do around the house and yard. He dug a garden and planted vegetables. He trimmed trees and fixed fences. He painted and cleaned gutters.

Don and I did not have any children, but he was a natural with mine and all the children of the extended family. He spent many hours of his retirement enjoying their company. When Eva was in grade school she would bring friends home to be entertained by Don telling his jokes. They were corny but fun and most of them were puns. Don loved playing word games with Bob and Eva. The kids laughed with delight.

One thing Don didn't give a darn about was his clothes. He had shirts he wore for clam digging that only had one sleeve. He didn't like the sleeve getting wet on his clam digging arm. Most of his working clothes were threadbare. Once he asked if I could patch a few holes. I was pleased to find colorful patches with patterns such as calico and various prints. And I was very proud of my mending. But Don came home from work after one day of wearing his newly patched clothes to tell me he couldn't wear them anymore. Seems the guys gave him a bad time about his colorful patches.

I would often pack a picnic for the two of us and off we'd go to Brown's Creek Campground or elsewhere in the backwoods of the National Forest. Don loved that. He would proudly tell me how many board feet of lumber were in each and every darn tree. He knew his trees like nobody else.

And we loved to go to Seattle for concerts by country western singers. We saw and heard Merle Haggard and Willie Nelson. What fabulous artists. And there was Dolly Parton. When she came on stage, the whole auditorium was filled with an instant "Ahhhh" from every male in the audience. I don't think they cared if she could sing or not. Once we heard Johnny Cash and June Carter perform an entire concert of songs about railroads. It was incredible.

Don would bring me a bouquet of freshly picked bear-grass each and every spring. The flowers of bear-grass grow tall stalks with many small flowers. Each flower is creamy white, saucer shaped, with a lightly sweet aroma resembling lilies, which they are. They were heavenly.

One night I came home from work to find Don in the bathtub. Come to find out his saw had slipped and gouged a large hole in his thigh. He informed me he was simply trying to soak all the sawdust out of the nasty cut so he could bandage it. I thought we should go to the hospital, but Don would have none of that. He soaked it and bandaged it and that was that.

Bear grass

I never received a Hallmark card from Don. He just didn't believe in them. But I treasure the orange sticky-note on which he wrote in pencil "Here is a beautiful lily for the love of my life, Billie! But buying a card by the ultimate Bard (me) seemed very foolish and silly. Xoxoxo Doenie!!"

Don would fall a tree exactly where he wanted it to go. He didn't second guess, he planned. He seemed to be able to communicate to the timber and give it precise instructions. Don and Carolyn Maddux had a predicament of encroaching trees on their farm property. One tree they wanted removed

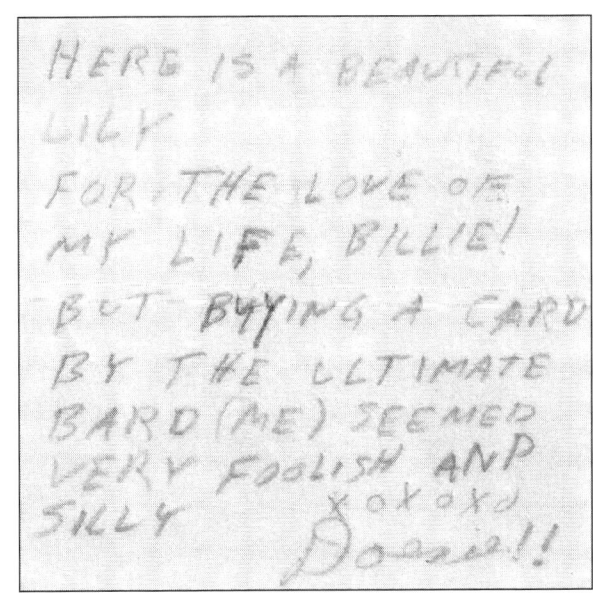

was so close to the fence that Don Maddux was prepared to move the fence out of harm's way. Don Howard thought that was a pretty silly idea, and just told Fr. Maddux to open the gate. He felled that tree precisely through the open gate, avoiding all harm to the near buildings or fence.

Don Howard was a true master of his craft. He always just believed he was only doing his job. His humility was one of his most endearing qualities.

Hunting season at the Howard household was always exciting. Don's friends would gather at our house before daylight to map out the day. I always had to pack a big lunch for Don because they planned to be gone all day – unless, of course, they got their deer or elk, whatever was in season. I would tell him I thought they were just going for a nice picnic in the woods!

If they were lucky, they would be home early and hang the deer or elk, skin it and let it just be for a few days. The longer it cured, the better the meat. Then the gang would return to our house to process the meat. Pat Carney, Greg Brown, Jack Mulligan, Laurie and Chuck Ward,

Don among trees

and others would all show up with knives in hand to butcher. Our ping-pong table was the center of all the activity. The wives and I would package and label the meat. Tons of coffee was consumed during this process. The back-strap always came to the kitchen first. It was my job to fry a batch of back-strap with onions so everyone could decide whether or not it was a good kill. When Bob wasn't hunting with his dad, he would join the crew around the ping-pong table. The cast of characters changed from time to time, depending on a person's schedule, but there was always a good time had by all. And the stories never stopped. I think some of them were just out and out lies!

About that ping-pong table: We bought an expensive and sturdy one early in our marriage so Don, a very good player, could play with the kids and his nephews. After all the kids were gone and Don didn't have his partners anymore, we just folded one half of the table up against the wall. Now it became a convenient place to plop bags of groceries as I emptied the car from shopping. And it served as a handy laundry folding table too. When it was to be used as a meat cutting table, I covered the table top with thick layers of newspaper, then I laid heavy duty plastic for under the numerous meat-cutting boards. Our ping-pong table served us well.

Once Don took a trip with Cary Settle to Canada to hunt moose. They had a great time and Cary actually got a moose! When it was time to do the cutting on our ping-pong table, Cary and his wife brought their young son with them. The son wanted to be of help so was given the job of labeling the packages. We all ate "mouse meat" for a very long time!

In the summer Don would take his nephews Tim, Doug, and Richard together with Bob and Eva and her friends, to Snow Lake to fish. Getting there was rather a steep climb into the foothills of the Olympic Mountains. The trip was always a summer's highlight. Bob loves hiking to this day.

# 7

Don and I had been married for about three wonderful years when my elderly parents' declining health forced them to sell the farm. They sold the house, barn and eleven acres to my nephews, Evan and Art Tozier. The remainder of the land was divided into three parcels for us three daughters. My oldest sister, Bernice, had the first choice and decided on the parcel by the river. Betty chose one closest to the house. Neither of my sisters had any intention of living or building on their parcels. But Don and I were thrilled with the third parcel of about six flat acres that fronted on West Skokomish Valley Rd. It was perfect for building.

So we had a comfortable two-story house built on this property. Moving in to that house was my homecoming. I could see the river and the two farms of my childhood from the windows in our new home. I had returned to the Valley.

Our Valley home

Don had taken over the care of Brit, a beautiful Brittany spaniel, given to Eva as a puppy. Don had big hopes of training Brit to be his hunting dog, but Brit was only interested in hunting the neighbors' chickens. He was the gorgeous color of a newborn calf's hide and so closely followed us around that we never had to put him on a leash. Perhaps we should have occasionally. Paul Hunter had temporarily left the hide of a young dead calf on his property. We found Brit busily chewing on that hide in the comfort of his dog house. Don retrieved the hide and apologetically returned it to Paul. And Brit loved the chickens! One day Brit came home with a live chicken from the neighbor's farm gently held in his mouth. Before returning the poor chicken to the neighbor, Don scolded Brit harshly and sent him to the dog house. I've never seen a dog pout like Brit did that day. Brit became a lap dog after he got shot running out of someone's chicken house!

Bob and Brit

I continued to be employed as the high school secretary. However, in 1962 the building that housed Irene S. Reed High School was deemed unsuitable due to age and deterioration. So the school functions, staff and approximately 900 students were moved to the Grant Angle Building at Ninth and Franklin Street in downtown Shelton. I was very annoyed with the way the school district handled the relocation. The office staff was left to move ourselves in our own cars. I am not sure how many trips I made loading and unloading, but it was too many.

My real love in this job was the students. I particularly enjoyed chaperoning on bus trips to various activities. Mrs. Ruth Willard and I had a great time chaperoning the high school band on a trip to Victoria, B.C. to participate in a parade. And the "rooter buses" were a hoot. I cheered right along with the students on our way to and from games in places like Port Angeles and Bremerton. But if I saw necking going on in the back of the bus, I'd just go sit beside the two smoochers. That would stop that.

I was more than a secretary. I was a friend and confidant to the students. Girls would tell me of their fear of getting pregnant. Or I'd hear sob stories about broken hearts. Kids shared family problems with intense feelings. When I detected the odor of marijuana on some of the boys, I wouldn't hesitate to get in their faces to tell them how obnoxious they smelled. We celebrated successes too. I'd be the first to give a "high five" for a good test score.

Bob graduated from high school in 1973, and Eva changed from Southside to the Hood Canal School District. It was about this time that Eva and I made our first trip to England and Germany, just the two of us. We arrived in Rochester, England, to be greeted by our relatives on my mother's side. We loved each other immediately. And the family resemblance was

Eva and Grandma Eva at the Berlin Wall on a return visit in 1979.

obvious in our shared sense of humor. Both Eva and I will always remember the amazing roses and the extensive variety of flowers in the neighborhood gardens, in addition to the gracious hospitality shown to us. We continued our trip to Dortmund, Germany, to meet my father's family. Fortunately Helga, the wife of a cousin, spoke English and acted as our interpreter. I remember our trip to a local carnival event. Helga ordered each of us a sausage sandwich from a street vendor. I found it to be quite tasty, although somewhat spicy. Helga enjoyed a good laugh telling me it was made from horse meat. We toured both sides of the Berlin Wall. The people in East Berlin looked shabby and needy with sad faces. Those in West Berlin appeared cheerful and happy as they crowded fancy sidewalk cafes and noisy night spots.

During the time when Eva was in high school, Don and I became involved in a 4-H student exchange program. That brought us Herath, a twenty-year-old from Sri Lanka, who was studying to be an agricultural extension agent in his country and was here to observe our customs.

Don and Herath in the forest

He was a young man of small stature with dark brown skin. We all gulped when he arrived at the breakfast table barefooted and wearing only a colorful sarong. He came from a well-to-do family in his native land, with parents who drove a Mercedes and farmed only with elephants. Their business was raising large crops of anthurium flowers they sold to buyers in the Orient.

Eva took him to high school with her and gave him the experience of American classes. Don took him to work for a day introducing him to the forest. He also took him fishing, although that wasn't very successful. Don said Herath spoke like an English peasant.

Herath stayed with us for a month on two occasions. We all thoroughly enjoyed the experience. And I remain in touch with him and his family.

So our good life continued on in the Valley. Don and I reconnected with my childhood friends and we continued our close relationships with old neighbors in Shelton. We had great neighbors in Skokomish Valley as well. Debbie and Rusty Baskin, who live in the original Latzel Dairy house, were right around the corner. Debbie had a large and wonderful garden. She shared her vegetables with The Saints' Pantry on numerous occasions. They named their daughter Sunshine. And Evan and Art Tozier and their families were within sight of our home as well. Good neighbors, good friends and nephews, of course.

In 1974, the Irene S. Reed High School, now called Shelton High School, moved to a new Mountain View campus of numerous separate buildings. It also expanded to a four-year school, including ninth-grade students and teachers. The school district, for whatever reason, reduced the office staff, thus increasing my workload. Part of my responsibility during the summer was to receive new textbooks and distribute them to appropriate classrooms and teachers. This required pushing large, heavy carts filled with books from one building to another to another. Counselors had their offices in one building and teachers were in buildings scattered across the campus. I walked back and forth between buildings all day.

I was getting tired. My legs ached and walking for any length of time became painful. My right leg was particularly troublesome. Lifting or carrying wasn't easy any more. I finally went to see my dear friend, Dr.

Doris Wilson. She grew up with me as Doris Hunter. She diagnosed me immediately with Post Polio Syndrome. I believe she is the only doctor who would have recognized the symptoms then; now it is more widely acknowledged. She not only knew me when I had polio, but she also had practiced medicine in third-world countries where it was prevalent.

In about forty percent of childhood polio cases, Post Polio Syndrome symptoms appear thirty to thirty-five years later. Sometimes it doesn't appear for fifty years! There is no test for it, and there is no cure. Unfortunately it is a progressive weakness and increase of pain in areas not originally affected by the polio. The Syndrome is a breaking down of the muscles and nerves that took over for those damaged by the polio. An interesting statistic is that the majority of polio patients have a "Type A" personality. We can handle it.

Dr. Wilson referred me to a Post Polio Syndrome Clinic at the University of Washington in Seattle. I went numerous times to see a young therapist at this clinic who eventually fitted a brace to my right leg for easier and less painful mobility. He spoke highly of a therapist he had interned under during his training, and how deeply he was inspired by her. During the course of our conversation, we discovered that he was speaking of Miss Brask – my therapist when Mother took me to Seattle as a young polio patient.

My job was not fun anymore. I was feeling overworked and underpaid. And my body hurt all over. I knew in my heart that it was time to retire – so I did in 1975. I was getting paid $650 per month. The school district had to hire two gals at $1000 a month to replace me.

Don wanted me to stay home and just enjoy myself. It was the first time in my life that I did not have to work. It sounded wonderful to me. I could have long and chatty lunches with friends, and devote more time to my 4-H club, which I loved. I had decided to start another club in the Valley with ten members. Pretty soon we had twenty members, and I had to seek the help of co-leaders. Helping 4-H members prepare to attend Panhandle Camp was a delight. The camp had grown to over 450 acres from the twenty acres it was when I attended as a young 4-H member. That camp will always hold a special place in my heart.

I loved the Grange and had been a member since 1976. I always helped plan the Skokomish Valley Grange community picnic – and just about anything else they wanted to do.

My mother was always active in the Veterans of Foreign Wars and Veterans of World War I auxiliaries in honor of my father's service. I played chauffeur on many occasions, driving my mother and her friends to conventions all over the state.

Concerned about not earning social security as a self-employed logger/worker, Don dissolved Howard Cutting and went to work for the Northwest Timber Division of Rayonier in 1978. He proudly held the title of bull buck. Don was assigned work in Quinault, about ninety miles from home. Some nights, he would just stay near the job rather than having to make the long trip home, especially in bad weather. It was a good job and he loved it, but it would have been much nicer if it was closer to home. We endured, however. Friends owned a cabin about a block from the Quinault Lodge. They graciously let us use it often, lessening our time apart.

Our cabin

As fate would have it, we were

given an opportunity to buy that little cabin. We jumped at the chance. It was wonderful. No TV. No phone. We could watch big herds of elk graze, and go fishing in the Quinault River. Walking in the rain forest was a delight. Every stranger we encountered soon became a friend.

The Saints' Pantry Food Bank began in 1982 in the St. David's church building. It got my attention immediately and I quickly volunteered my services. Every Monday and Tuesday, I'd help unload cars and trucks full of donations, sort food, and prepare it for distribution. It wasn't the smartest thing for me to do physically, but very emotionally rewarding. Then on Tuesday night or early Wednesday morning, I would drive to the cabin. Sometimes Don and I would come home to the Valley on the weekends. Eva was now in college, so it was just the two of us. We had the best of everything.

One day Don's aunt, Emily Babcock, presented me with a two-dollar membership in the Mason County Historical Society. She had a motive: She felt that being of mature age, she should no longer drive and wanted a chauffeur. So I began to drive her to the meetings and attend them as well. At that time the meetings were held in the small museum located on the fairgrounds by the airport. Maybe there were a hundred registered members, although only a few dozen usually attended. They were talking about my town, my Valley and my land. And everyone, including me, discovered that I could contribute a wealth of historical information. The society and I fell in love. I never missed a meeting.

It was not long before I was approached by Irene Davis, the director for the society. They needed a volunteer to accept, itemize and catalog incoming material. She thought I would be perfect and easily talked me into the position. So on Fridays, I began to do just that.

Anyone who knew me quickly became aware that my church and its ministries were – and still are – a large part of my life. Supporting the food bank, doing numerous secretarial duties, organizing activities that supported the good of humanity, teaching Sunday school, being a Youth Advisor, serving on the Vestry, being a Convention delegate and just about anything else St. David's needed was always a high priority. In 1986 I was extremely humbled and honored to receive a Bishop's Cross from the Diocese of Olympia. I was blessed.

Now I had a time-juggling mess, with my commitment to the 4-H club, food bank, the historical society, St. David's Church, and Don in the cabin in Quinault. But never letting much bother me, I stayed organized in my busy world. I was happy and fulfilled.

The cross is silver with a Bishop's Crozier in the center. A simple strand of rope is used as the necklace. The Crozier or staff is a reminder of the Bishop's need to keep watch over his flock.

Dick Brewer, president of the historical society, somehow managed to talk the city of Shelton into giving the society a 25-year lease for the empty building on the prominent corner of Fifth and Railroad in downtown. The building was built in 1914 as Shelton's city hall and library. This beautiful building was absolutely perfect for the historical society.

My legs were now getting a lot worse. It got to the point where I could not perform the physical requirements of my volunteering at the food bank, even on a minimal level. It was time to give it up so I regretfully did . My focus then became the Mason County Historical Society. The director, Irene Davis, a Belfair resident, no longer wished to travel back and forth, so she stepped down. Guess what? I happily took her position as director in 1990.

I had a great time setting up the museum's new home. It was not a quick and easy task. The location drew lots of attention from the community. People quickly began to bring huge quantities of material that had been stored in attics and basements for decades. I welcomed the pictures, documents, and items donated. The history of the Valley and Shelton was becoming more vivid each day.

Soon I was hired to open the museum two days a week. I was actually now earning a salary for my passion. It delighted me when old timers came in to share their stories, or a great-grandson came asking when his great-grandpa taught school here. Sometimes I was asked if I recognized anyone in a dated black and white photo. I loved the research projects. I was always informing or learning.

Two Squaxin Indian brothers, Randy and Jim Krise, went to the Ming Tree restaurant down the street from the museum at exactly four o'clock every Friday evening. One day I was standing in front of the museum and caught their attention as they walked towards the restaurant. I asked them if they were aware of the extensive material the museum had on Henry Krise, their ancestor who settled in Kamilche. They were not, and they stepped into the museum for a detailed history lesson. The next day two cars crammed full of young Krise descendants visited the museum with a great deal of enthusiasm and interest in learning.

To this day, I wholeheartedly thank my old boss, Dave James, for all he taught me. Being his secretary while he was the public relations director for Simpson was one of the most valued experiences in my life. My tasks in that position prepared me for my proficiency at the museum. Conversing with people, researching material, organizing and writing for publication has served me and the historical society well. Staff and volunteers in the museum increased. Membership in the Historical Society increased. I continued Irene Davis's monthly newsletter, writing articles of the past, present and future.

Don and I smile for the camera at Twanoh State Park on the Canal.

# 8

Don retired in 1994, and soon we sold the wonderful cabin at Quinault. Our Valley house became our full-time residence.

One day we got the bright idea to purchase a used American Clipper 32-foot cabover motor home. At the time, we thought it sounded like a great plan. We would just go traveling all over and enjoy our life as RVers. Well, that proved to be one huge mistake! First of all, neither one of us really enjoyed traveling, at least not for extended periods of time. And we had bought an older model RV, 1976 to be exact. Lucky for us, we stumbled onto a group of American Clipper owners who formed a club called the "Evergreen Clippers." They were all retired folks, just like us, who really didn't like to go very far from home. What a blessing! We learned that American Clippers were collector RVs, not made any longer, and of a really good fiberglas construction on a Chevrolet or GMC body. We had bought a classic! The best time we had

Some of the "Evergreen Clippers" vehicular members.

in the ten years with the Evergreen Clippers was when fourteen of us entered the Fourth of July parade in Forks, Washington. We decorated each RV with red, white and blue bunting, hung appropriate signage and drove the parade route as a group. We camped in the yard of one of the RV owners, ate, played cards and just had a good old blast. We also took a couple of trips as a group to Wenatchee, the Long Beach Peninsula, and Chehalis. It was fun while it lasted, but I was glad when it was over. The motor home was eventually sold at an auction for St. David's Church.

Bob earned a degree in Forestry from Centralia Community College in 1975. He fell in love with airplanes at his college job with Twin City Airways and went on to obtain his commercial pilot license. His job took him to Alaska where he met and married the love of his life, Karen Kavinsky. She had two teenage daughters, Gillian and Sylvia, and the family settled in Anchorage. They lost the oldest daughter, Gillian, tragically to leukemia in 1996. Sylvia is a physician's assistant and married to Brian Okuley, and

Max Calcagno, Karen and Bob Godwin, Jeff and Eva Calcagno, Fletcher Calcagno

they too live in Alaska, in Chugiak. Bob and Karen are both anticipating retirement in the near future.

It was when Bob left our home that we took custody of Bosco, an Australian shepherd Bob had raised from a pup. Bosco constantly had a Frisbee in her mouth, begging someone to throw it for her. One winter's day, I took Bosco to Graves Creek Campground for a good dose of exercise. There were not any campers there, but the park ranger came along to make sure Bosco and I were okay. I threw the Frisbee for Bosco – and she joyfully returned it to me – for the better part of a day. When we returned to the car, I discovered it had a flat tire. Of course the park ranger had long gone and I had no choice but to change the tire myself. Bosco patiently sat at my side and watched the ordeal. The spare tire was those funny little ones designed for very temporary use. Don was quite upset with me for being at the campground alone, and rather surprised I managed to change the tire. He took the car to the gas station for repair the next day.

Brit and Bosco were my farm companions. Often I would pick corn for the Toziers in the summertime. These two dogs would patiently sit at the end of the row of corn I was working. When I finished the row, I'd shuck a couple of ears of corn for Brit and Bosco who would hold the corn in their front paws and eat the entire ear.

In 1985, Eva earned her master's degree in library science from University of Washington, where she met her future husband, Jeff Calcagno, in the same graduate program. Currently she is Cooperative Library Services Manager for Washington County, Oregon. Jeff and Eva's oldest son, Max, attends the U. of W. and their younger son, Fletcher, entered high school this year in Portland.

By the way, remember my friend Beverly Rosenberg? Well, she married my ex-husband, Frosty Godwin. Small world. I think they were happy.

Frosty died in 1989. Bev and I are still friends to this day.

I always looked forward to the Forest Festival and parade every spring in downtown Shelton. When I worked at the high school, I served on the committee to select Paul Bunyan, the Forest Festival queen, and her court. My nephew, Art Tozier, was Paul Bunyan once and my great-niece, Julie Johnston, was a princess. I've only missed two festivals in my life. The theme for the 1999 Festival was "Our Heritage." You could have blown me over when I was voted by the Forest Festival Committee to be the Grand Marshal. I was the very first woman to receive this honor. It was one of the biggest thrills in my life to ride down Railroad Avenue in the official convertible, with so many people waving and calling out my name. I saw many folks who had played a part in my life: 4-H kids, high school students (all now adults), family, friends, and neighbors both past and present. My 99-year-old mother rode with me in the car, having the time of her life. My entire family lined up in front of the museum waving and shouting as we rode by. We celebrated the event at a family picnic at the PUD Park on Fourth Street after the parade. What a wonderful memory.

Waving to the crowds as the Forest Festival Grand Marshall.

My mother's one-hundredth birthday party was terrific. Family arrived to celebrate the occasion from Canada, England, Germany and the USA. We had cousins by the dozens, some we had never seen before and some we didn't know existed. My mother was a trooper through it all. Betty and I

Mom surrounded by 100th birthday-party guests, all relatives.

hosted the two events. The first one was held in the afternoon of October 7 in St. Edward's Parish Hall for the many friends she had acquired over the years. The second was a sit-down dinner prepared by a caterer for over one hundred guests – all related. It was held at St. David's Parish Hall in the evening. Queen Elizabeth showed up (played by a Canadian cousin) to welcome the guest of honor and delivered a proclamation from the actual Queen, brought by the English cousins, for the celebration. It was a lot of fun.

The following day we all gathered at Evan Tozier's home in Skokomish Valley and enjoyed salmon from Alaska and beef from the Valley barbecued outside, accompanied by music and visiting. Evan's home is located on the Weaver Creek property previously owned by my parents. It was a very appropriate ending to a great weekend.

So life is good, and life goes on, and we get older.

"Our Story," the book my mother wrote.

My father resided in an extended care facility after selling the farm and property. He died in 1977. Mother lived on the farm for a short time and subsequently moved to Fir Tree Park in downtown Shelton. She wrote a book, when she was one hundred years old, and passed away at the age of 104.

On March 17, 2005 I was presented with a Mason County Heritage Award by the Mason County Commissioners, Jayne Kamin, Lynda Ring Erickson and Tim Sheldon, for my work at the museum. Also receiving awards were Bruce (Subiyay) Miller of the Skokomish Indian Tribe, Charlene Krise of the Squaxin Island Tribe, Bill Somers of Grapeview, and Rand Iversen of Matlock. It was humbling to be included with historians I admired and appreciated for their work in historic preservation.

Our Austrailian Blue Heeler, Reno.

We gained another little furry friend after Betty and Bud Tozier returned from a Christmas-tree selling trip in Las Vegas. An old Australian Blue Heeler crawled under their trailer and would not leave. The Toziers felt they had no choice but to bring the dog home, which they did – and then gave him to Don. We named him Reno. Reno followed Don everywhere, and particularly loved the hikes on Mount

Ellinor. Reno was always one foot behind Don. If Don stopped, Reno stopped. One day Don commented that he must be getting slower because when he slowed down, Reno would now walk around him, find a place in the shade, and just sit and wait for him.

Don continued to hike, fish, and hunt with Bob, nephews and friends. He cherished hiking to his "secret lake" each summer and being the first to cast a fishing line. He had backpacked fingerling trout to it sometime earlier and enjoyed observing their growth and the ultimate catching of them, too.

"Mr. Elk" was Don's greatest achievement as a hunter. Hunting with friends in the Four Stream area of the Skokomish, he shot a large elk. It had to be packed out and wheeled out in a wheelbarrow by several of his friends. It was towards the end of Don's capabilities as a hunter so it was a really big occasion. We did the usual hanging, skinning, and cutting up processes, but then had to decide what to do with the head and the antlers. So Don enlisted the talents of Roger Samples, a taxidermist in Shelton. "Mr. Elk" never looked so beautiful and dominated a large portion of the family room in our home in Skokomish Valley.

Above: Fizerinkum the cat naps on Mr. Elk.
Left: Don packing out his hunting prize.

After the kids grew up, Don would spend much of his time at the Purdy Canyon Drive-In, where he loved to eat, and entertained folks with logging and hunting stories. He and the owner, Carl Kvarnstrom, would go razor-clam digging each season. I never could understand the thrill of driving clear to Ocean Shores, sometimes in the middle of the night, in order to get there by daylight to dig a limit of 15 clams. But the guys had a great time and it gave them something more to talk about.

Don had been retired for about ten years when I first began to realize that he was beginning to fail mentally. Alzheimer's came on so gradually, it took quite some time before I was aware of what was really happening. He began to forget how to start his power saw. Sometimes he couldn't find the keys to the pick-up, so he would drive the riding lawn mower from our house to the drive-in. He would forget to put a belt on his pants. He wouldn't remember what I said or would repeat himself. Just little things at first, things I know I should not have ignored. We laughed about it, but the concern was growing.

Then prostate cancer struck. I had to fit Don's doctor appointments, treatments, and surgery into my schedule. I wanted to blame his confusion on the cancer and drugs.

Flood damage in the Valley.

An infamous flood hit the valley in 2007. Don did not have the mental capacity to move the cars out of danger. The waters flooded our home. It was horrible, the reality of every Valley resident's nightmare.

Our vehicles stuck under water during the 2007 flood

Paul and Leslie Hunter lived just across the road. The day after the flood, Don had to go to St. Peter Hospital for scheduled minor surgery. Our car had three feet of flood water damage, but the pickup truck was parked on higher ground and had not been affected. We got loaded for the early morning trip to Olympia and discovered the pickup had a flat tire. Here came Leslie, keys to her SUV in hand. She loaned her car to us for the day and we made the scheduled surgery time for Don. Bless her heart.

When we returned from the hospital, Don wasn't allowed to do any heavy lifting. Here came Chase Hunter, Paul and Leslie's son, every morning to get our firewood so we could dry out our basement. Bless his heart.

Chase also climbed the ladder to our two-story home to spray the yellow-jackets' nest in the eaves. It was a scary task, but someone had to do it! The Hunters also had a daughter named Allison.

I won't even go into the pet deer that they kept in their yard until she got too big and too rambunctious to keep.

Shortly after the flood, we realized we had no option but to move. So Don and I sold our property to the Tozier boys and closed the wonderful chapters of our life in the Valley.

We bought one of the three homes for sale in Christmas Village, a retirement community of individual homes in the heart of Shelton. It was a perfect location for Don to view the comings and goings of life from the comfort and safety of his living room chair.

However, our new home just couldn't accommodate "Mr. Elk." We would have had to cut a hole in the ceiling for the antlers and his head would stick out too far in the room. "Mr. Elk" now presides at Tozier Brothers Ace Hardware Store in downtown Shelton. I believe Don is happy to know he is once again on display.

I continued to work at the museum. I needed to work, but it was difficult as I would have to come home periodically to check on Don. My great staff was very supportive and understanding.

Then in 2008 I received an American Business Women's Award from the Mason General Hospital Foundation. Every year the foundation honors three businesswomen who are or were successful in their occupations, or who have been or are currently working or volunteering in Mason County. Also receiving awards were Pam E. Hanson, owner of Cameo Boutique and Wine Shop in Union; and Laurie Buhl, Heritage Bank Senior Vice President in Community Lending. It was especially nice that Pam Hanson was a student worker for me in the school office when she was in high school. It was great fun to be included with these two young businesswomen in receiving this prestigious honor.

Don passed away in October of 2010 at the age of 82. He enjoyed his good life to the fullest. A part of my heart died with him. I will always miss him.

I retired from my position at the Mason County Historical Society in 2011, at the age of 76. My post polio problems and the need for a younger, stronger director were the deciding factors.

My friend Marilyn Lear was now Marilyn Miller. Life had given her many challenges since the last time I saw her. Her daughter had lost a leg to cancer as a teenager. Marilyn and Charlie had divorced, and some time later she re-married. Marilyn lost her son in a deep-sea diving accident working for a salvage company in the Atlantic Ocean. Marilyn's husband had also recently passed away. So, when Don died, Marilyn came quickly to my rescue. She was most helpful in the months following his death and during the grieving process. And, lo and behold, she returned to Saint David's Church. Oh, we discuss world problems, gossip, eat out and work on church projects. I am grateful to Marilyn for her friendship through the years. Neither one of us has much money, but we don't need it to laugh.

The Skok Valley Class of '46 gathers at the Irene S. Reed High School 60th class reunion. Left to right: Fred Sjoholm, Annette Bienek McGee, Arlen Johnson, me, Bob Wilson, and Roger Richert

Skok Valley friends and neighbors at the Valley community picnic in 2012 include from left to right: Carol Hunter Taylor, Doris Hunter Wilson, Darlene Moore Wilson, Karen Ragan Ramsfield, and in back, Zanie Campbell Crowe and Colleen Campbell Kallappa.

Today, I am busier than I have ever been in my good and blessed life. I enjoy activities involving the historical society, the food bank, both Skokomish and Pomona Granges, PEO, and my church. I keep active, but on my own time and in my own way. I'm not too good at saying "No," but getting better with "I'll think about it."

I visit with my daughter and her family frequently, and she often makes the trip from Oregon to be with me. I speak to Bob frequently, although our visits are few; we try to get together once a year.

Nearly every year, I am personally invited to be a guest at high school class reunions. It is always such a pleasure to be with the adults I knew as students. I love knowing of their lives today. I attend lunches to celebrate birthdays with my childhood friends. It seems there is always a wedding of grandchildren, or a birth of a great-grandchild of one of my many lifelong friends. The funerals are the hardest. So many goodbyes. But no matter where I go, I am greeted by someone I've known for oh so long.

I am surrounded by love and laughter.

Life is good. The magic of the Valley continues.

A view of the Valley circa 1980.
Billie and Don Howard's Home
Weaver Creek Farm
Latzel Dairy

# In Billie's words
# 9

*I guess it is appropriate to say that if I had it do over, I'd probably live my life pretty much the same way. Only, perhaps, I'd have handled my divorce from Frosty better. It wasn't pretty, but it was necessary. I hope and I think my children have forgiven me. We are still good friends. It's funny, how life changes a person – we grow up at the most inopportune times! By the way, they are both "the adults" and I am "the kid" or so it seems now at my age of 79. I ask them for advice.*

*I couldn't have had better parents. Sure, they were so busy all the time making a living that they didn't know where I was or what I was doing most of the time. But they let me grow up in my own way, create my own style and live my life accordingly. They didn't pity me one bit through the polio years – I had to do my share of the chores and they supported me through thick and thin. Thank you, Mom and Dad.*

*My sisters? They raised me too. Bernice and Betty are both gone now. I literally grew up with their children. We lost Cathy Moorhead but Joyce, her sister, and Maxine, Art, and Evan Tozier are still in my life, as are their children. For that I am thankful.*

*And my grandchildren. Karen's daughters came into my life when she married Bob in 1995. They were teenagers. What lovely girls. I keep in* touch with Sylvia and her husband, Brian. Sylvia is a physician's assistant in Chugiak, Alaska, and Brian is a teacher.

Eva and Jeff Calcagno have two sons – Max and Fletcher. What joys they are. Max is presently taking chemical engineering classes at the University of Washington. He graduated from Wilson High School in Portland, Oregon at the very top of his class, and Fletcher entered Wilson High School this fall with a straight A average. Both boys play piano. Fletch also plays the trumpet in the school band, and sings in the choir. He earned the "Best Eighth Grade Boy Musician" award in his school.

Now for Don – we had two months shy of 40 good years before he died. I wish he could have lived long enough to enjoy Christmas Village with me. It is a great place to live. Don supported me, encouraged me, laughed and sang with me through those almost 40 years. He was a good stepfather to my kids and I think they both appreciated him. I miss him dearly and I still talk to him, believe it or not. The "Frozen Logger" was his favorite song, so to his memory, I'll leave you with this verse:

> My lover was a logger, and not just a common bum
> Cuz no body but a logger stirs his coffee with his thumb!

The extended families in my life all took me in and accepted me, warts and all.

Now, there are three Episcopal priests who have played a big part in the development of my life. Without the church, I couldn't have got through it. There is an old country and western song that has a line in it "Drop kick me Jesus, through the goal posts of life" – and I think He has. The church has always been there for me.

**Fr. Clarence Lody** and his wife, Isobel, saw me through the divorce. They provided support when I needed it and didn't hesitate to withdraw it when *necessary.* **Fr. Don Maddux** *and his wife, Carolyn, married us, got us through the years of raising the children and provided a friendship that I will cherish forever. And* **Fr. Joe Mikel**, *and his wife, Nancy, came into my life after Don had passed away and helped get me back into church activities that had been cast aside during Don's long illness. They made me feel whole and useful again.*

*And, to Irene Davis, the former museum director, I give thanks. She saw something in me I didn't know existed. I knew nothing about museum work until she retired and literally gave it to me. She laid the groundwork for the Mason County Historical Society Museum – all I had to do was do it. She made it easy for me. And to Mike Fredson: when I got discouraged and thought it would be better if I quit, he asked me "If I was still having fun?' I replied, "Well, yes, but that's not the problem." He quietly said, "You don't quit as long as you are still having fun." So I stayed another ten years.*

*Do you remember my mentioning George Hermes and David James early in my working life? Well, I had the occasion of working with Mr. Hermes again at The Saints' Pantry – he was a volunteer and he picked up bread from stores for distribution to the clients. And, Dave James, a historian who has written several books and publications for the Mason County Historical Society, came back into my life at the museum. What goes around, comes around. Living in a small town isn't really all that bad.*

*I can't go any further without talking about the staff and teachers at Shelton High School. They were dedicated people, fun to work with and for. We laughed and cried together. Floy Batstone, who I worked with the longest, was a good friend. When talking about her husband, she would start with "Jim said." Oh, by the way, he held the patent for the clam gun – you know, the round tube you put in the sand, and up comes a clam. There were Pat Connolly, who I still visit with on the phone from time to time, remembering all the crazy stuff that happened; Mary Littlejohn – the same*

Mary Kneeland Shelton Littlejohn who took care of me when I was a child – took care of the attendance. I had graduated with her son, Leroy Shelton in 1953. Donna Nutt – what a great gal she was. Her life ended much too soon. When folks asked her about her name she always replied "that's Nutt, with two Ts." And the staff: Reta Loudermilk – a former teacher of Don's – and I chartered an airplane from Twin City Air in Chehalis to fly over Mt. St. Helens after it blew; Nora "Pat" Newman, who I took typing from in high school, became a good friend. She lived to be 105 years old. Oh, yes, I returned to SHS to haunt Irene Burright, who flunked me a semester in business education. And Carole Howard? She became my sister-in-law!

After George Hermes left SHS for Garrett Heyns High School at the Washington Correction Center, Clyde Brown took over as principal. A nice fellow but he longed for his eastern Washington roots and returned to Brewster and became a Superintendent of Schools. Chet Dombroski, my former U.S. History teacher became the principal as well. They're just a few of the folks I worked with and associated with during my career as high school secretary. It was an interesting time – all fifteen years of it.

Several classmates get together each month at Rooster's to eat lunch and visit. This has been the most rewarding time of my life as far as keeping and creating friends. I actually don't know how it started except that Myrna Wallin Bennett must have had something to do with it. The last Monday of each month you can find us at Rooster's – Myrna, Annette Bienek McGee, Dorothy Morgan Durand, Selena Lane Myers, Adella Carlson Dwyer, Gerry Haugen Himlie, Lena Wingert Tober, Marian Ashford Eveleth, and Barbara Bailey Pyle; and when they are in the area, Pat Hunter Smith and Rea Berry Brown drop in. Lately, a brave fellow, Jerry Sheldon, has been participating along with some of the husbands. The best part of this story is that in high school, except for a couple of us, we were not friends at all. But, now at 79 or so years, we are. How good is that?

*I can't sign off on this book without mentioning my museum staff. None of us started out with any background in museum work, but we sure learned fast. Shirley Erhart has become about the best researcher ever. It it's there, she'll find it. Shirley actually worked in the museum before it was a museum – The Shelton Public Library. Jan Parker is a magician with the picture collection and Stan Graham, retired from the Forest Service, could find anything on a map. Both Parker and Graham are involved in and knowledgeable about historic preservation. Elsie Parker, who drove back and forth from Victor in North Mason once a week, took care of the memberships. Charles Fisher and David Larson filled in wherever necessary. And Justin Cowling came to us when he was 16, volunteered to do whatever needed to be done, and hung around until he is now the director. Not one of them worked full time, but all were essential to the operation of the museum.*

*The volunteers: I can't praise them enough. Too numerous to identify, they did everything else – baked pies for the car show, sold books at the Mason County Fair, Matlock Old Timer's Fair and Oysterfest; catalogued and filed collections and artifacts – you name it, they did it! They were great to work with and never said they couldn't or wouldn't.*

*Our board of directors is a pretty complex group as well. Led presently by Annette McGee (yes, the same Annette I went to school with and was an attendant in my wedding to Frosty) has a wealth of knowledge useful to the Society from her work as a County Commissioner; Del and Barbara Griffey, a husband and wife team from Allyn, have been working for and with the MCHS almost since it began; Frank Gray hails from Hoodsport and has been serving for a long time as well; Peter Replinger of Cloquallum, our resident railroad historian, is valuable in that area and has written a book and several articles on Mason County railroads; Vern Rosenberg lives at Mill Creek but his roots go back to the Agate and Skokomish areas; Ray Kimbel, valuable as a car-club member, is also a member of the Kimbel family that provided construction work and logged in the County, as well as* *one off the founding families of Forest Festival; Tim Anstey, from Union, provided valuable input but has recently resigned and turned his chair over to Steve Bloomfield from Kamilche, whose roots are deep in the shellfish industry. Dave Valley recently joined the board as treasurer. Then there's historian Michael Fredson, a past president, a cheerleader and a promoter of the Mason County Historical Society and what it stands for. His books are too numerous to list but he has documented almost every part of Mason County and is presently working on <u>The Sustained Yield Contract, Public Law 273</u>.*

*That about does it. I have left out a lot and probably put in things I shouldn't have, but it is basically my life. I grew up at a time when things were simpler, life was safer, and Skokomish Valley was a magical place to live and grow up. The potlucks at the Grange Hall and the reunion of school and Valley folks each summer are important to me. People and relationships are important to me. I love it all and I hope you enjoyed reading about it.*

**This book is dedicated to everyone and anyone who touched my life and made it enjoyable. Like I said, "If I had it to do over, I'd do it all again."**

*Billie*

# About the Author

Susan "Suzy" Petty and her husband, Mike, enjoy life in Shelton. She is an on-going participant in "Anyone Can Write" taught by Carolyn Maddux at Olympic College. Suzy's favorite hobby is listening to delightful stories while taking abbreviated notes and then devotedly creating the life story of a remarkable person.

# Author's acknowledgements

First, I acknowledge Billie Howard as someone I highly admire, deeply respect and simply love. Thank you, Billie, for telling me your story. My profound thanks to Carolyn Maddux for her constant encouragement, on-going education, and repetitive edits that I am sure frustrated her, and most of all, for her faith in me. I acknowledge all my friends who lovingly nudged me with their frequent, "How's the book coming?" And my beloved husband, Mike, who never groaned when I asked him to read a chapter one more time. Thank you, Mike, for your amazing patience, honest feedback, unwavering enthusiasm and loving me even when I was consumed with writing. Colleen Scott Design was a new experience for me. Colleen took my many pages of typing and professionally turned them in to a book. Thank you, Colleen, for your magic. Thank you, Billie, for this amazing experience. This is my gift to you, your family, and everyone who knows and loves you.

**Suzy Petty**

# Afterword

*The Magic of the Valley* was printed in Luxi Serif, a baroque style typeface designed by *Bigelow & Holmes Inc.* at the beginning of the 21st Century. Page and cover design was by Colleen Scott of Colleen Scott Design. Unless otherwise noted, photos in the book are from Billie Howard's collection. The back cover photo was taken by Myrna Bennett.